STARTING THERAPY

– A BOOK FOR NEW THERAPY CLIENTS –

ALISON CROSTHWAIT

©Alison Crosthwait, 2017

Published by Alison Crosthwait

All rights reserved. No part of this publication may be reproduced, stored in a retrieval system or transmitted, in any form or by any means, electronic, mechanical, recording or otherwise (except brief passages for purposes of review) without the prior permission of the author or a license from The Canadian Copyright Licensing Agency (Access Copyright). For an Access Copyright licence, visit www.accesscopyright.ca or call toll free to 1-800-893-5777.

Library and Archives Canada Cataloguing in Publication

Crosthwait, Alison, 1975–, author
   Starting Therapy: A Book for New Therapy Clients / Alison Crosthwait.

Issued in print and electronic formats.

Cover Photo: Milada Vigerova https://unsplash.com/@mili_vigerova

ISBN 978-0-9947871-4-9 (paperback). – 978-0-9947871-5-6 (epub). – 978-0-9947871-6-3 (kindle)
   1. Psychotherapy – Popular works. I. Title.

This is an original print edition of *Starting Therapy*.

This book is dedicated
to my clients.

CONTENTS

Introduction — vii

Chapter 1 – Thinking About Starting — 1
Why you might enter therapy — 1
Is it time to begin therapy? — 6
Is psychotherapy effective? — 8
Finding a therapist — 10

Chapter 2 – Starting — 15
Shame and Stigma — 17
Advice for starting therapy — 19
Poetic Aside: Why people are scared of therapy — 21

Chapter 3 – The Basic Set-Up Of Therapy — 25
Time — 27
Money — 31
Talking — 35
Boundaries — 52
The end of the session — 55

Chapter 4 – Digging In — 57
Cultivating Change — 57

Poetic Aside: What it feels like to change	67
Thinking	69
Feeling	76
The Unconscious	79
Projection	83
Your relationship with your therapist	87
Our Development	95
Difficulties in therapy	96
Should you stay in therapy once the crisis that brought you there has passed?	103

Chapter 5 – Final Thoughts — 105
Complementary Practices	105
What is emotional health?	107
Resources	119
Acknowledgements	121
About the Author	123

INTRODUCTION

Most people enter therapy with a vague sense that it might be worthwhile.

We meditate to become calm, we work out to lose weight, gain strength and live longer. We all have a pretty good understanding of how things like meditation and exercise work. But how does therapy work?

In therapy we want to relieve our suffering, break patterns, and change into the people we know we are but just can't seem to be. What is not always clear is how these changes might occur.

For myself I had no idea of what might actually happen in therapy when I began.

Now, many years later, I have some understanding of the range of possibilities available in therapy. Of what can be accomplished. Of what could happen for you. But I don't know everything about your therapy. You'll craft your own experience. This book is just a nudge at the beginning of it all.

Therapy is a strange thing in a way. And not at all in another.

Conversation comes naturally to most humans. We long for it and we seek it out.

A gifted therapist who is the right fit for you can help you change your life. Together you can discover possibilities, feel the pain and joy that has been bottled up, and wonder together at the human condition.

To begin therapy is to start a new relationship. Possibly one of the most important of your life.

This book outlines many things that may help you as you begin therapy.

But I have a serious caveat to everything I am about to say.

Imagine a book on dating with a set of rules. Many such books exist. What use is this? Most people in a long term relationship will tell you that what makes a relationship successful is identifying what works for the two parties in the relationship and their own unique way of being together – not an external set of rules. A rules-based approach to finding love and staying in love leads to anxiety and a prolonged period of masking on both parties. A lifetime partnership is formed in a myriad of ways. A book may give you an insight or framework that is helpful but the relationship is yours.

So too therapy. Therapy is a relationship. This book outlines some ideas and resources for the relationship. The intention is not to provide a set of rules by which you measure your own therapy or therapist. The intention is to shed light on various areas that could be of help for you to think about. But it is your path. You and your therapist's.

When you have done some work in therapy you will come back to this book and say – she was wrong about this, and, I wish I had noticed this chapter.... And if you are reading this now as an experienced patient you will see yourself in it in places and you won't in others.

I hope this book stimulates your thinking. I hope you ask your therapist many, many questions. And I hope you ask yourself a fair number too.

I believe that this world would be a richer, and more compassionate place if therapy was better understood and more widely practiced. I write this book in the hopes of supporting the practice of digging in and working through. Of breaking cycles and patterns and starting anew. Of loving this life and this world for the wonder that it is.

CHAPTER 1
THINKING ABOUT STARTING

Why you might enter therapy

You are suffering. Something in your life is not working. And it is causing you pain. Or at least you have a lurking feeling that something isn't right. That's why you're here. That's why you're beginning (or thinking about beginning) therapy. And that's why you're reading this book.

You want a change. You want life to be better.

No one person's reasons are the same as another's.

If you stay in therapy for any length of time it is likely that your initial reason will change and your reason for staying will not be the same as that at the beginning.

STARTING THERAPY

Issues are not discrete. Depression, trauma, grief, insecurity… they are words we have for certain experiences and feelings. But we are whole people who can't be separated into parts. All the issues and strengths form a whole, and the whole is what comes to therapy.

So I would say – hold your "reason" lightly. It is a very good reason. And there's more. And the answers won't be what you think.

It might help you to hear some of the many reasons to begin therapy that I have heard. Some are situations, and some are feelings. Some come from a negative place – not wanting something. Others come from a positive place – wanting to move towards a brighter situation. Some involve you as an individual, others are about relationships. No two are ever the same:

1. I am serious about living a good and meaningful life and am grappling with what that means.
2. I have started a new romantic relationship and I want it to go well.
3. I have started a new job and I want it to go well.
4. I am stuck on one event or relationship and keep ruminating about it over and over.
5. I see myself repeating the same patterns in my romantic relationships and don't know how to break the cycle.
6. I can see that my success is limited by a trait in myself – perhaps a fear or a worry – something stands in the way of my growth and I want to overcome it.

7. My relationships at work are having a negative impact on my job performance.
8. I got a performance review that raises questions of how well I work with others and something about it rings true.
9. Things are coming up in my meditation practice that I want to explore.
10. Despite continued attempts, I cannot quit smoking, reduce alcohol consumption, or lose weight.
11. I have more to say than family, friends, and colleagues have time to hear.
12. I have tried all the self-help books but have ended up back in the same place.
13. My spouse is overwhelmed by supporting me through this phase.
14. I find myself feeling outside my life – not fully present – something has changed, and I am not sure what.
15. I feel stuck in an important area of my life and don't know how to move forward.
16. I am having difficulty dealing with my in-laws and don't want it to impact my marriage negatively.
17. I have more to do than I can possibly accomplish and can never seem to right the ship.
18. I find myself irritable, angry and sometimes even tearful at home or work or both.
19. As a parent, I worry about how my stress is impacting my children.
20. As a parent, I worry about repeating my parents' mistakes.

STARTING THERAPY

21. As a step parent, I struggle with how my spouse and his or her ex are parenting the kids – and I wonder what is at stake for me in this dynamic.
22. I have suffered a loss – a death, a divorce, a job.
23. My relationship is in turmoil, and I can't decide if I should stay or go. And how to proceed in either case.
24. I am having an affair, and I don't know what I want. Or why I did this. Or what to do.
25. I have trouble focusing.
26. I have trouble being alone.
28. I have trouble being with others.
27. I have one or more unexplained physical ailments and wonder if they may have a psychological connection.
29. I or someone I love has a chronic or terminal illness.
30. I am a caretaker for someone with a chronic or terminal illness.
31. I am struggling with infertility.
32. I have sexual difficulties – physical or emotional.
33. I want to kick an addiction.
34. My partner says I drink too much and it causes conflict between us.
35. I want to get healthy.
36. I have chronic health concerns (for example pain or fatigue) and I want to learn to cope better and explore the possible emotional roots of them.
37. People say I talk too much.
38. People say I am emotionally unavailable.

39. I am attracted to emotionally unavailable friends and lovers.
40. I have suffered a trauma and want to finally deal with it. Trauma can be anything from an accident to abuse. Trauma can be witnessing an event or experiencing something yourself.
41. I am depressed. I am having difficulty enjoying life or even getting out of bed.
42. I am struggling to manage my anxiety.
43. My anxiety is so bad I have had panic attacks recently.
44. I can't sleep.
45. I hate my job and don't know what to do.
46. I am trying to make a big decision, and I want help weighing the options.
47. I am overwhelmed with being the caregiver to my children and/or my parents.
48. I am struggling with destructive eating patterns or I have an eating disorder.
49. I am struggling with the meaning of life and asking existential questions which I do not find others in my life able to engage with.

You can see that the range of issues is vast. Usually, it is some difficulty or unfilled desire that takes us to the next level of our growth. This thing is the door to the next phase or chapter of your life.

Is it time to begin therapy?

Are you on the fence about starting therapy?

I encourage you to give yourself a chance. To step into a therapist's office and give yourself the chance to talk to someone.

To talk about everything that is on your mind – what the holidays were really like; how you feel emotionally and physically; what life is like with your spouse, your kids, your work and your boss; what you are worried about.

Your life's purpose. Your life's meaning. What you really want. What you hate. All the things you think you can't tell anyone.

Give yourself a chance to open up to someone who is trained to receive in a different way than our culture usually receives. The right therapist won't reflexively 'take your side' or offer you sweet sentiments just to appease. The right therapist won't be quick to judge. And the right therapist won't jump right in and tell you what you should do or what you are like. The right therapist for you listens and receives and responds from a human place with their training and experience on their side.

Give yourself a chance to break your patterns. To emerge from the ties that bind you. We all have such incredible potential. It's hard to see when you're not living it. But it's there. Give yourself a chance to work with someone who can see it even when you can't.

Therapy makes a difference. Every hour when a human being is heard, when a person is allowed to be who they are – every hour this happens the world opens up just a little bit.

You might be frustrated at how long it seems to take. That therapy isn't a "cure." But, hour by hour, give yourself a chance.

Perhaps therapy is a bit like deep tissue massage for the soul. It can be intense. And you feel it afterwards – sometimes for days. But all this intensity didn't come from nowhere. You were already carrying it, and perhaps you had been for a long, long time. Through therapy, it has been drawn out. You need to rest and nurture yourself. You are healing a bit, and becoming a little more whole. A little more directly aware of yourself and what you have experienced: the good and the bad.

So why not? There may be many good reasons. And you have to work with those reasons. Therapy may not be your path, and that is how it is.

What we all consider in some form is this: every day you make active choices. So you're on a path. You're in something. We're in something. And reckoning with this is something. It's something you do – you have no choice but to keep going on that path. The only question is how.

From what I write it is probably clear to you that I see psychotherapy as going beyond mental illness. What do I mean by that? I mean you don't have to have an addiction or a disorder to benefit from psychotherapy. Psychotherapy at its best is an opportunity to grow that uses our strengths as well as the areas that are more difficult for us.

If you are considering therapy, I hope this book helps you understand the practice of psychotherapy and helps you decide if it is your path. I hope it proves a foundation and a jumping off point for your work. And I hope it inspires you – because so much is possible in this practice.

Is psychotherapy effective?

The easy answer is: yes. Research shows that therapy helps to relieve depression and anxiety. It is effective in treating a range of conditions including addictions and trauma.[1]

But even as I write this I feel uncomfortable.

Therapy is not an external process that is "done to" you.

Therapy alone can't help. Therapy cannot take place in and of itself. Therapy is a process in which you and your therapist engage. There is no therapy outside of you, the client.

So if just turning up to therapy itself can't help, what can?

What can help is you and your therapist engaging in the process. It's not a small difference.

---

[1] For example: The Efficacy of Psychodynamic Psychotherapy, Jonathan Shedler, American Psychologist, February-March 2010 available at jonathanshedler.com

There is nothing passive about psychotherapy. It is much more similar to training for a 10k or starting a fitness program than it is to taking a drug. The comparison between therapy and drugs is a comparison of two drastically different ways of being for the patient.

Often these two alternatives are presented as options – as if a doctor could either give us a pill or put us in a therapist's office. This dichotomy underlies so much of the misconception around therapy.

To present medication and therapy as equal alternatives is to imply that psychotherapy will be done 'to' you. Just like most things in our culture. Sit on this beach and have your vacation done to you. Get in this car and have the experience done to you. Buy a ticket and let the movie entertain you.

As if you – your desires, foibles, insecurities, and loves – as if you have nothing to do with what the picture looks like. When in fact – you *are* the picture.

Successful therapy requires your investment.

What does investing in the process of therapy look like?

It looks like: going to regular appointments, speaking your thoughts and feelings, and trying to take in the experience – however it is for you. There is no one right way. Your therapist can not tell you how to feel or how to respond. Investing in therapy is engaging with yourself and your therapist in a process that is aimed at your well-being.

STARTING THERAPY

Finding a therapist

It can be difficult to find a therapist. Most people struggle with this part. The mental health system is complicated and varies greatly depending on where you live. It is so important to find a therapist with whom you feel comfortable and safe. Someone that you like right off the bat. Someone who can help you move forward. Who can challenge you as well as reassure you.

The really difficult thing about finding a therapist is that when you are trying to do this you are perhaps not at your strongest. You are going through something. You may be in a deep crisis. You may be in a low mood. Either way, you're not at your best.

Advice for finding a therapist

Ask some people for referrals in your area. Some people that you can ask include teachers, religious leaders, doctors, or other holistic or alternative medicine providers. These people are likely to know some therapists to whom they can refer you. You could also ask people you know who have been through something difficult and come through the other side in a way that inspires you: a loss of a loved one, a divorce, an addiction, an emotional crisis. These people may have a therapist to recommend or ideas of who to ask.

Think through the people you know in those categories. Contact one or two of them and ask them for suggestions of a psychotherapist they would recommend. You don't have to say it is for you. But if you can be open with them about your situation you will get a more personalized response.

Be choosy about who you ask. Ask someone you respect who you feel will keep your confidence and work in your best interest without judgment.

I strongly recommend this method of asking trusted people for referrals. In today's world, however, I know that most people find their therapist online. I understand the pull. You get anonymity. And instant gratification – you can search and then contact someone directly.

But if you can – and I know it is difficult – ask people that you trust for help. The ability to market and the ability to work with people as a therapist are two very different skill sets.

Once you have some names, look them up online and get a feel for them. Does what they write resonate with you? Keep in mind what I said about marketing. An aging website is not an indication of a poor therapist but rather a therapist whose attention is not focused on the latest in web design. Slick marketing is one thing. Words that move you are another.

Then go to have an initial consult and see how it feels.

It is often a good idea to meet more than one therapist for an introductory consultation. This will highlight the differences between them and help you make your choice.

Specialties

Therapists often list specialties. But often as prospective clients we don't know the specialties we need. When I entered therapy, I would never in a million years have thought that trauma work was something I needed from my therapist. Now I know that it is. So unless you are absolutely sure you need a certain speciality, I would focus on finding someone you feel you have a good fit with and who believes they can help you rather than looking for self-diagnosed specialities.

I have also come to believe in process above all. Every situation is different. Specialists are valuable in some cases, but transformation is personal. No two people are alike.

There is lots of good information available about modalities if this is important to you.[2] I have not gone into it in-depth because I believe the quality of the practitioner and their fit with you is the most important thing to focus on as you chose a therapist. And the work of the practitioner on their self. I talk about this in the next section.

I assume in this book that you want to do some deep work. That you are looking for more than a few sessions to get you through a difficult time. Given this, it is much more important that you find someone with whom you have a good rapport. Someone you feel comfortable with, can laugh with and cry with. Someone you feel gets you. These people exist in all of the modalities.

---

[2] For information on the many types of therapy see www.goodtherapy.org/learn-about-therapy/types

The most important thing

The most important thing is that the person you work with has and is doing their own personal work.

This is a big part of the reason why I don't suggest choosing a person by modality or specialty. The important thing is that the person you are working with continues to struggle with themselves. Continues to experience the humility of being vulnerable with another person.

This can take the form of ongoing therapy (which I believe all therapists should have been in for years). It can also be supervision. Or other forms of healing and growth.

If a therapist has not looked at themselves, they will not be able to help you look at yourself.

That is not to say that the therapist must be perfect, have life figured out, or know everything about the areas in which you struggle.

But they need to be in touch with their humanity. They need to know what it is like to struggle. They need to know when they need some help themselves. They aren't likely to share this with you but it is part of the ground that supports your work in therapy.

Ask a prospective therapist about their own development and how they do their own work nowadays.

CHAPTER 2
STARTING

This can be a very awkward time. Or intense. Or anxiety-ridden. Or none of these. It depends.

It depends on you and what you bring, and on your therapist and how she works.

Some therapists like to take what we call a history. They may take notes as you talk and they may have many questions about your life, your family, and your relationships. In this way, they build up an understanding of your background.

Other therapists work by starting where you are and let the details emerge over time, creating the picture through what you say and what you don't say.

Personally, I make the decision depending on the client. If I feel that I need the information to understand what is happening, I will ask many questions and take a formal history. If the client is having trouble getting started, I will ask questions as prompts to help them begin to open up and talk. If the client comes in with a specific issue at hand that is emotionally intense for them that will become our focus. In that case, I won't take a formal history, instead I will piece details together as they come up.

I follow the client because the client knows what they need to heal. Not consciously, perhaps, but their whole being knows. And the project is to bring the healing momentum of the individual to their awareness. I do this initially by not interfering with it.

Every person is so different. What they experience and what they need is never the same. Your therapist is trying to understand you. Don't assume she knows everything. Especially not everything about you. Help her out and tell her whatever you are aware of. The more open and honest you can be, the more you will help your therapist, and the more she will be able to help you.

You are also free to have your privacy. You don't have to tell her everything. The key question is: Why am I choosing not to say something? Is this reason worth exploring?

And ask all the questions you want. Even those you don't want to if you can. It's the beginning of a relationship and talking about what you are thinking and wondering will build a strong foundation of understanding, equipping your therapist to really help you.

So bear with the intensity. Allow yourself to feel the discomfort that arises. Talk about it. And say whatever is on your mind.

Shame and Stigma

To go to therapy is to admit you need help.

All of us need help. In lots of different ways. We need people to grow, harvest, process, and sell our food. Many of us have massage therapists, personal trainers, and doctors.

But when it comes to therapy many people feel they are weak if they need it. That they are somehow sick or crazy because they are struggling with something to do with mental or emotional health.

When you have an infection, you go to the doctor, and you know they will give you antibiotics. When you have a broken limb, you know you will get some kind of cast. But when you are confused or grieving or depressed or anxious and you go to therapy: what are you going to get?

The treatment, so to speak, is unknown. And the reasons for your distress and troubles are often unknown. There's no clear answer. Things can't be given a number, weighed, quantified and systematized. You can't say that X is wrong and the remedy is Y. And so sometimes it is easier to just avoid the whole thing.

STARTING THERAPY

It is understandable and normal to be nervous about entering therapy. To worry about your mental health. To feel unsure as to what lies ahead.

Be assured that by addressing your problems you are entering on a new path of learning about yourself and others.

People from all walks of life have found therapy to be a crucial part of their lives – there is no one type of person who comes to this practice. As stereotypes cross your mind – feel free to challenge them and see them as information about your feelings about your process.

You don't have to tell everyone or anyone what you are doing. There is no rush, certainly.

Over time, you will find those people who are interested in having the types of conversations you are interested in having. Who want to open up and explore. Or you will enjoy having a private world that is just yours.

You are up against something big in this process of trying to make a change. You are up against the way things are. Most people function within the status quo. Acceptance is how our world works. It's just easier. You will have to lean up against the tide of your life, including that of the people around you. You will have to push against it ever so slightly to begin to ask yourself questions about yourself and others and how your world works.

Anxiety around what people think might be difficult for you. Coming to terms with something that is yours and yours alone is a big part of the work. The process of coming to terms with what people think of you (including you being in therapy) is an integral part of therapy.

So if shame comes up about the fact that you are in therapy – talk about it in therapy. There is likely to be a lot to explore.

Advice for starting therapy

Here are some thoughts about beginning therapy:

The process of therapy will involve the unexpected. You don't know the answers. That's why you are coming to therapy. Not to be given them, but to explore them. Being prepared for this at the outset can make the surprises a bit less disturbing.

Ask questions. There are so many different approaches to therapy. And each therapist and client build their own relationship and process together. You have every right to know what is going on and what to expect. Ask whatever you want. You and your therapist are dealing with your life, after all.

Therapy doesn't feel good all of the time. You arrive in therapy because something isn't working. You are suffering. You want something about your life to be different. To get to 'different' you will in all likelihood have to dig deep and go through a significant personal process that may involve more pain at first rather than less. The process varies for everyone. But most agree that it is hard work and requires courage and persistence.

Expect resistance – from yourself. Beginning therapy puts all of you on alert. By saying you want to address things about yourself you are letting yourself know that you are watching and that you care. This can inflame your issues and anxieties. They may be screaming out for attention. Expect parts of yourself to act out, be self-destructive, and generally resist the process. You, the adult who has made the decision to get serious, need to meet the resistance and bring it to therapy to be explored.

Be kind to yourself. Find a way to take care of yourself as you begin this process. Is it 10 minutes of journaling at your favourite coffee shop after sessions? A steam at the gym? A walk through the park as the leaves turn? Make time for just being in your week, just as you make time for therapy. Therapy is work. Hard work. Building kindness around yourself will provide space for that work.

Like anything, hard work and perseverance pay off. I used to think I wasn't a runner. I couldn't run. Then a friend told me about slow running. And I tried it. And I liked it. And eventually, I ran a 10k. And then another. I'm not a serious runner, but I can't say "I don't run" anymore. Therapy is similar. You come in with ideas about yourself. If you find a way that works for you, and if you stick with it, your view of yourself and your experience will change. In ways you can't imagine when you start.

Poetic Aside: Why people are scared of therapy

I woke up this morning in the grip of a panic. I hadn't felt this way in years. The feelings were so strong that they seemed to be the truth. I felt in my body like I was in imminent danger. That everything was going to be taken from me.

My heart, stomach, torso-it was like they were gripped by iron clenches.

Of course, I had just woken up in my same bed, with the same set of good and bad life circumstances I had yesterday. But the feeling was one of risk.

There have been times lately when I have congratulated myself on all the good work I have done. I have been in therapy for years and have been growing and deepening as a clinician and person. I have been through a very difficult phase and I feel myself healing ever so slightly. I feel more grounded and less ashamed.

And then this morning – clenched. Unable to focus or breathe or speak.

It is true that I have worked hard, and now, much of me is well.

But when overwhelming feelings burst through it is a reminder of just how much sits below our conscious awareness all the time.

There is terror. Rage. Grief. Joy.

All of this sits under there, in our unconscious. And for good reason.

Sometimes it seems unsafe to feel these feelings. We are taught not to feel joyful. That there's a risk with feeling sad. Or, don't, at all costs, show your anger.

Feelings do not define us. Sometimes we resist feeling what we consider to be negative feelings such as anger, envy, or sadness because we fear we will be "an angry person." We all have a full range of feelings inside us and no single feeling defines us.

Sometimes we seem to have no emotions at all. We unconsciously keep our feelings buried, and then the feelings come out when we're least aware, or in the form of compensatory behaviours that aren't good for us, or chronic health problems.

So when we treat therapy like a hot potato, tossing it aside with criticisms such as –

"I would never pay someone to listen to me."

"That industry is a scam."

"I can't afford it."

"I don't have time."

"I don't see what it's doing for me."

When we say things like this, most often (although not always) we are jumping away from emotions that are just too much for us.

Because who would want to actually feel that clenching terror I woke up with? Who would make an appointment to explore these things? Who would deliberately open themselves up to such a thing? Who would choose to feel it again, voluntarily?

Way worse than the dentist. Seriously.

The flaw in this reasoning of avoidance is this. Although we may not consciously be aware of our emotions all the time, they still are in us. The terror that has nothing to do with my current daily reality. That is something I carry. In my cells. In my being.

The only question is how we are with ourselves. That is what we get to choose.

If, for a moment, we can catch ourselves shunning and avoiding our feelings and rest for just a moment; if we can resist the belief that we really are too busy or we really are in danger and rest in the feeling for just a microsecond; if we stop running away and face things, however briefly... something might happen.

We might see ourselves.

We might be seen.

We might breathe for just a moment.

STARTING THERAPY

We might let the chair we are sitting in support us.

We might shed a tear. Or smile.

We might let something out.

My experience is that we continually sell ourselves short. Our understanding of what is possible is almost always smaller than what is truly possible.

There is a lot more possible for us than simply not feeling as anxious. Or feeling less depressed.

The paradox is that by feeling worse, we get closer to the experience of being human. We have to let in the things we don't want to feel to be able to feel all the things we do want to feel. When we do this, we are expanding and blooming in our full range. We can't muscle ourselves into blooming in only one direction. Numbing the bad also results in numbing the good.

Great joy and great rage and great energy and great sorrow are all part of life as it exists. We can't get around it.

Because we're in it.

Throw the potato when it's too hot. But if we can hold it long enough to see what it feels like and how hot it really is, well, this is when it gets interesting.

This is when we start to change.

This is when life begins to happen.

CHAPTER 3
THE BASIC SET-UP OF THERAPY

One of my teachers tells people starting therapy that they have a "duty of honesty." That, as much as possible, they should try to be honest with themselves and with their therapist. And that, if you really allow yourself to struggle, feel it all, and speak what is on your mind, everything will unfold from there.

We have everything we need. We just need to pay attention to ourselves. Remove the blocks. Stop hiding behind the falsehoods just because they are easier. We need to do this over and over again. And in the case of therapy, in the presence of another who is also paying attention.

This is the basic set-up. Bring yourself – however you come – and talk about what is happening for you.

STARTING THERAPY

The Frame

Another part of the basic set-up is what therapists call the frame. The frame refers to the practicalities of therapy – where, when, how often, how much, etc. It includes time, money, confidentiality, your therapist's office, and boundaries.

Each therapist is influenced by their training and their background and they create an environment that works for them. They create a frame that allows them to work with you in the best way possible.

Some therapists vary the frame for each client. Some do not. There are few hard and fast rules about the set-up.

Your reaction to the frame is meaningful.

By paying attention to what happens within and around the frame, you and your therapist can learn a lot about you and your relationships. You can probably dig into material that is related to the reason that you came to therapy in the first place.

Do you make your appointments well in advance? Or do you leave it until something bad happens, and you want to talk about it?

Do you have a regular time?

Do you call your therapist? Email her? Text her?

Do you pay before your session? During? Weeks later?

Do you feel comfortable in the room?

Do you resent the bill, or see it as an investment?

All of this is meaningful. It is all part of your relationship with your therapist.

The frame is the embodiment of your therapy. It is how you and your therapist actually do this thing. How it is set up.

The frame is what is happening around, behind, below, and above all the talking.

In a sense, the frame is the therapy.

If you have questions, thoughts, feelings about any of this – talk away.

It's a duty of honesty that gets us where we want to go.

Time

"Everyone knows it takes three to five years of weekly sessions to effect change," a colleague said recently.

You will most likely experience benefits right away when you start therapy.

And you will experience ongoing change and insight all along the way.

But deep work takes time.

STARTING THERAPY

You are bringing a lifetime of experiences – physical, emotional, and spiritual – to an hour of work a week.

Deep work takes time.

How often should you go to therapy?

The usual concerns I hear are with regards to time and money.

My usual response is that it is a better use of time and money to come every week than every two weeks. And overall I believe this. I would rather someone come weekly for six months than every other week for a year.

But this is a very general statement.

Each of us has different needs, different psychological makeups, and different nervous systems.

In general, coming to therapy more often helps unconscious material rise to the surface more quickly. If you go on a trip with a friend the little things that bug you will result in a fight. If you see them once a year that won't happen. Frequency brings feelings to the surface so they can be worked with. And the more often we see someone, the more we get to know each other and the deeper the bond we can build. We build trust. And knowing. Which leads to insight and growth.

Regular therapy also helps reduce anxiety about the process as you get used to the sessions more quickly. You build your relationship with your therapist more quickly, and she gets to know you better so she can help you more effectively.

Regularity also helps ensure that habits and changes are being reinforced rather than lost between sessions.

I had a client who struggled to commit in her relationships. I had the sense that if I asked for too much of a commitment (and that is how I felt she would hear it – me asking and she giving) that she would flee therapy. I told her every other week was just fine. And we have been working for two years and made excellent progress at that frequency. Asking her to commit weekly would have sent her running. I could feel that. She needed to work at her own pace.

And so like everything in therapy the right frequency is different for everyone. People have different relationships to time. There is no one standard.

What matters is if the therapy is meaningful to the client and to the therapist. Together, client and therapist decide on everything including how often the client comes to therapy.

The usual paradox of working on ourselves applies here. We need to push ourselves. But not so much that it's too much. In terms of frequency of therapy I am regularly checking in with myself with each client – is this too much? Not enough? If I think a change might be of benefit, I'll bring it up, and we can talk about it together.

A regular time – whether weekly or fortnightly does seem to help clients and the therapist settle into the work. Although again that's a general rule.

STARTING THERAPY

The question I have for you the therapy client is: what frequency do you think will help you address your issues best?

Watch out for the inner reasoner who has reasons for everything. Time and money can be defences against deeper feelings. Give these deeper feelings time to come out – talk about them. And together, with your therapist, make the decision.

I also think it is important to consider what the rest of your week looks like. There are many complementary practices to therapy, and I'll talk about these later in the book. It's like going to a trainer. You go once a week, but the rest of the week you sit on your couch and eat junk food. You probably won't get the results you want.

Learning and growing is a process. We have a natural tendency to back away from what is most difficult, and we are endlessly fascinating in the ways we convince ourselves that we don't do this.

The practice of psychotherapy is a practice. Like any work that we do. Spiritual. Physical. Emotional. Any practice deserves our best.

And what the best is is yours alone. There is no measuring stick. Some people come to therapy for one session and do what they need to do. Some of us work for years.

This is the work of therapy – to come in contact with yourself and to learn something from that place.

So deciding on frequency with your therapist is a significant part of the work. Worth careful consideration.

Money

This is a stressful topic when it comes to therapy. And complex.

Every statement we make about money ricochets with our history and our being. It is important that we treat our thoughts and feelings about money the same way we treat our thoughts and feelings about anything else. As things to be learned from and reflected upon.

With money, we have to do two things: deal with its reality and hold it as an energetic and subjective experience just like any other.

Paying for therapy

Therapy is an investment in yourself.

When I was worked in a corporate job I made a good income. Therapy was completely affordable. Yet I still thought it was expensive. I did it, but something about it felt – extravagant? Now that I am self-employed as a therapist my income is much lower. And I still go to therapy. My old self would have said I couldn't afford it. Now I see it as crucial to being who I am. My whole economic scale has been adjusted.

Note that your scale may need adjusting.

STARTING THERAPY

What are you worth?

I think of the client who comes to therapy having difficulty in her relationships with men. She wants a family – a husband and children. And to date has chosen men who are uninterested in commitment. What is therapy worth to her?

The client dissatisfied with their work.

The client who can't get over the loss of their mother.

The client who drinks too much.

The client whose anxiety causes him to turn down a promotion.

Addressing these problems has to happen for these lives to get better. There's no limit on the value of a life.

I know that I should have a lighter touch sometimes. I know that people will find their own way. But I find it so difficult to see people edge around their suffering.

Because the end game isn't good.

I see that personally. And I see it in my clients.

Loneliness, depression, ill health, bitterness, and boredom. People whose later years are just not good.

I didn't know life could be good. I didn't know it could be rich. And these discoveries propel me to describe the ways we express our lack of self-worth in our proclamation that therapy is expensive.

We wouldn't dream of asking a surgeon to work on us for free. But it is difficult sometimes to wrap our head around paying our therapist. I think looking at it in terms of a doctor is helpful in this case. You want someone well trained. And well compensated. Because you two are going to work on the most intimate parts of you.

These are the things at stake when we think about paying for therapy. If you find yourself ready to leave therapy on account of money I strongly encourage you to take a session to talk about this with your therapist.

The economic reality – therapy is expensive

Many many people cannot afford therapy. For so many reasons.

It is not an equal playing field when it comes to the availability of therapy.

And it is also true that there are many possibilities for obtaining therapy when you can't pay.

Here are some ideas for where to get therapy at low cost:

- Training institutes often have clinics for low-cost therapy
- Graduate student clinics
- University clinics

- State funded medical care
- Non-profit clinics for specific issues such as eating disorders or victims of violence
- Places of worship and religious organizations often have counselling services

If you can't find care – ask people you meet what they suggest. Contact community leaders, mental health bloggers, and educators in your area. Ask for suggestions of where to find therapy at a low cost.

It may take some time and perseverance but consider your statement "I can't find affordable care" to be a perspective rather than a fact.

What can't you find? What haven't you been able to find? What has happened in your life when you have needed help? How might you be repeating this scenario? In your search for a therapist, begin to think therapeutically. See yourself as a person who is suffering who deserves compassion and keep working on your own behalf.

I'll also say this: An earnest request from someone who wants to work is worth a lot to me as a therapist. This is the work I am trained to do. I love what I do and want to work with clients who value that work. My colleagues and I invariably keep a portion of our practice on a sliding scale. And we regularly make referrals to low-cost alternatives. It's amazing what can happen when you ask.

Issues can arise around the timing of payment, mode of payment, and cancellation fees. Keep an open mind and be curious about what is being created or repeated here between you and your therapist. These behaviours might indicate something in other areas of your life. For those of us with money "stuff", there is a deep well to dig here.

Talking

Preparing for your therapy sessions

So you're in. You've started. You have therapy today. And you don't know what to talk about.

Things clients often say:

"I didn't prepare anything to talk about today."

"I don't know what I am going to talk about today."

While these words mean something different every time in every person, often I hear in them shades of self-criticism and judgment.

As if they should have prepared. As if they should have done their homework. As if not knowing is somehow wrong.

I am one of those people who is pretty good at preparing. I create deadlines, schedules, and detailed plans. These are important to me. They allow me to stave off the humiliation that comes from being unprepared. They help me hold myself

STARTING THERAPY

together and keep pushing forward. They present the image of someone who is just fine, thank you.

My planning, organizing, goal setting, and calendar management also support my delusion that I have it all figured out. And if I have it all figured out, nothing can happen to veer me from my path. This is good because to veer from my path might involve loss, shame, attack or humiliation and I don't want to feel those things.

But the veering is also life. Life as in all of the emotions and experiences of being a person. Life as in the creativity of writing and speaking and moving as we are. All my (our) planning can foreclose that.

And when my clients and I chide ourselves for lack of preparation in therapy or make a preliminary disclaimer as if to say "I am not responsible for what happens next – I didn't prepare"... I know we are missing something in that moment.

How does one prepare for therapy? I don't think lists and plans help much here. Marketing writer Seth Godin's words are appropriate:

> We are unprepared to do something for the first time, always.

> We are unprepared to create a new kind of beauty, to connect with another human in a way that we've never connected before.

We are unprepared for our first bestseller, or for a massive failure unlike any we've ever seen before. We are unprepared to fall in love, and to be loved.

We are unprepared for the reaction when we surprise and delight someone, and unprepared, we must be unprepared, for the next breakthrough.

We've been so terrified into the importance of preparation, it's spilled over into that other realm, the realm of life where we have no choice but to be unprepared.[3]

If therapy is about change, the best thing we can do is be unprepared.

Starting a Session

The first words of a session are important.

Often we minimize them. Small talk. Something unimportant.

But almost always they turn out to have meaning.

Many therapists don't engage in small talk at the beginning of the session for this reason. The therapist's reticence fosters the client's revelation – which is the focus of the therapy.

I used to work this way. I have come to believe, however, that the relationship is the most important piece. That some people value this so-called small talk as a way of connecting. Of feeling real and normal. Not speaking can be seen as aban-

---

[3] sethgodin.typepad.com/seths_blog/2015/01/unprepared.html

donment or distance or playing "the shrink." If the relationship is too badly hurt the distance is unproductive. I work to keep professional distance while staying close enough to be reachable. Human. And at the same time, I always note how we begin the session.

As a client, you too can be mindful of your beginnings. Of how you feel the night before, the morning of, the hour before, whilst in the waiting room.

All of this is meaningful and worth talking about.

What you say first is important, too.

As I've said above, often clients feel the need for social courtesies, particularly at the beginning of the session. They ask how I am. Remark about the weather.

This is fine.

But it's not necessary either.

As you start out, I want you to know that you don't have to greet your therapist in a comfortable way. You don't have to check in on her. You don't have to say happy holidays. It's all about what you want to do and say. That's what's important.

If you feel compelled to do something for an external reason, this creates an energy. This energy is important. It is likely present in other parts of your life. The impulse to take care of your therapist or make sure she is alright or some other type of pattern – this is golden information to work with in therapy.

Be aware of everything. Your impulses. Your words. Your interactions. It all has so much to offer.

Things you can talk about in psychotherapy

You can talk about the same thing every single session. Every single one. No problem.

You can talk about who you want to be in the world.

Your dreams, aspirations and ambitions.

You can talk about politics. About race and sexuality and gender. About your own biases and beliefs.

About sex too.

You can talk about money. Debt, inheritance, gains, losses. Salaries. Jealousies. Anxieties.

You can talk about your health and the health of those around you. You can talk about the intimate details of your body and the choices you make every day.

You can talk about what you eat. How? When? What do you worry and think about when it comes to your food?

You can talk about death. Deaths you've witnessed. Deaths you've feared.

And births. Births experienced but not remembered, births desired, births contemplated, births witnessed.

STARTING THERAPY

You can talk about the most (supposedly) boring details of your day to day habits.

You can talk about what impacts you. What you read and watch.

What you are afraid of – what petrifies you? You can talk about that.

If something seems too gross or too terrible or too trivial, that's something to notice.

A while back I wrote a list of all the things I didn't want anyone to know. I thought it would be a very short list – "I'm open," I thought. The list was long. And it wasn't a list that I could convince myself to talk about – they truly were secrets.

You can talk about that too. The fact you have secrets. Things you won't talk about.

You don't have to censor yourself in therapy. The more you can be honest the more value there is. And when we are reluctant or ashamed to talk about something it is useful to consider why. It's not that everything has to be laid out – having our private inner world is important – it's about examining what we share and what we don't share and why.

Therapy operates at multiple levels – it's about a lot more than "things to talk about." But the things are important. The things relate to your experiences and ideas and beliefs and values. The things and how you talk about them are so important.

You can talk about them all.

Some thoughts about talking in therapy

So much of what we say uses other people's words. Words we have heard. Things we think that we 'should' think.

We're buried so deep because no one has taken the time to listen. To draw out our own voice. The one that doesn't sound like anyone else's.

This sits on us like a weight. Our own voice deep inside as we repeat things we think we should say.

That's why talking down to someone or at them doesn't work when the goal is emotional health. Or any kind of authentic conversation.

It pains me more and more how much "talking at" exists right now. Real conversation involves talking with.

Advertising is an obvious example.

As is politics and the media. And social media. But we've taken it on, too. As healers. As friends. As lovers. As parents.

A conversation involves (at least) two nervous systems.

What that conversation feels like depends on the experience of both participants. The connection that they feel.

One of the richest discoveries in therapy for me has been the joy of conversation. Of talking with someone and putting my thoughts into words. The reward is hearing my conversation partner's response – how they put my words together and make sense of them based on what is happening for them right now.

When someone responds to your self from their self, it takes both of you somewhere new.

This is much more difficult than talking. This is talking and then receiving a response. It is listening to that response. It is perhaps interrupting our own train of thought or an exciting story to check in with the listener and see what is happening for them.

It's alive.

It's this aliveness that gets buried in the sound bites that replace real conversation.

In therapy we learn: we can listen. To ourselves and each other and all the beings with whom we share this planet.

And we can, as we choose, tell them who we really are. All the good bits, and the bad bits. The real bits.

And this will be rewarding.

During the session

One way of understanding what is happening in a therapy session is to use the concept of free association, originally developed by Sigmund Freud. The idea is to say everything that comes to your mind, editing nothing.

The idea is that by not editing yourself and letting the words spill out you reveal your unconscious feelings, wishes, desires, and fears which the therapist can then interpret back to you.

Interpretations are not necessarily correct. You and your therapist can then discuss and you both can reflect on what has been said – by both of you.

Saying whatever comes to your mind is extremely difficult. And it is only part of the picture of what is happening in therapy. The practice in its pure form is rarely done nowadays outside classical psychoanalysis.

That's not to say that we don't do it in therapy today – we just do it differently.

We do it when words tumble out. In our jumps from one topic to the next without an obvious logical connection.

Often people feel they have to be organized in their presentation of words. Like things have to make an argument or tell a story.

There's no point trying to make sense right away in therapy. The sense will emerge in time.

Bring yourself. Say what you want to say. Your being has brought you here – conscious and unconscious. Let it all speak. Sense will be made. Over time.

STARTING THERAPY

The best thing you can do is generously open your soul to the process as you feel able. Show yourself, and the pieces will come together.

Another way to think of this is like a dream. The session is a dream. It is an expression of your unconscious self wrapped around conscious facts, happenings, and actions.

Let it be as a dream. And what needs to come forth will come forth.

Sessions have many layers. Therapy has many layers. One way of conceptualizing what is happening during a session is to think of it as like a meditation. If you have ever attempted meditation you know: a lot happens when you sit still in silence! I have done multi-day silent retreats that were operatic in their content. The mind, body, and emotions are active. Your feelings will be making a lot of noise.

In therapy you are also watching yourself. You are expressing and being and seeing and wondering and letting it all come up. You are trying not to judge it but to be with it. And it is often uncomfortable.

It can be valuable to talk about therapy in therapy. To talk about what is happening in sessions.

For example, if you find yourself updating your therapist with detailed accounts of the time since the last session, a useful question might be: what are you trying to do in these detailed accounts?

It may be that you need to go to therapy more often because you have a lot to say and process and you are always playing catch-up rather than going deeper.

Ideally, you and your therapist are able to go beyond updates on events to an exploration of what is happening for you in your life, what isn't happening, and how you feel about it. And also to explore the dynamic between you and your therapist.

This takes a long, long time for many people. For very good reasons. Their relationships have been fraught with difficulty and talking about their lives is as close as they can get right now.

We can also use stories to distract from our deeper feelings.

As with everything in therapy – this is worth exploring for yourself and talking about with your therapist.

Technology During The Session

If you can, turn off your phone entirely.

The new smart watches are pretty bad for therapy. They are highly distracting.

Create boundaries so that something can happen in the room.

If you can, don't use your phone immediately before and after sessions.

Let yourself steep in the work.

I know this sometimes isn't realistic. I often can't do it either.

But the path of mindfulness is worth taking.

If you can create a boundary and seal it tight and say "This is my time. This is the time to work and explore and to be – without distraction." If you can do this for yourself it will be worthwhile. If you can't, that's alright too. But if you can – push yourself to turn off your phone, watch, emails, laptop – all of the distractions of life. And dive into the work.

Self Judgment in Therapy

I often listen, rapt, as a client says things that are important. New things I haven't heard before – clearer feelings, new connections. And then they something like – "I'm rambling." There is such a tendency to judge ourselves when we get into new territory.

This is worth noticing.

The new is always scary. Always. It couldn't be otherwise. And that's why you came to therapy. For something different. Something new.

What is Happening In Those Awkward Silences?

Shared silence can be many things: disturbing, awkward, terrifying, peaceful, romantic… the list continues.

I find that silence in therapy, particularly at the beginning of a therapeutic process, has a tendency to be disturbing and awkward, for both therapist and client. And I think this discomfort has something to teach us both inside and outside the therapy room.

Often I sense discomfort when the talking stops. Clients will often say that the silence is disturbing to them. Often it is difficult to get to the bottom of. People know they are disturbed but don't know the nature of it.

Sometimes people feel exposed, other times they feel uncomfortable. Ideas of 'doing therapy right' come up. Being under my gaze may be uncomfortable and thus another avenue of exploration.

As a therapist I want to leave room for my client's mind to wander, for a feeling to arise, for them to just be. But I don't want to leave them feeling abandoned either.

Anytime anxiety rises and/or we feel uncomfortable something is happening. It is a sign that we are on the edge of something.

Language is a safe place for many (although not all) of us. Ideas are interesting, our words entertain and engage, we are thinking and being all at the same time. Words fill a space. When language stops what is happening?

Stepping outside of language for a moment, however brief, takes us into new territory. In this new land we don't know what will happen. We create the opportunity for something new if we can bear our discomfort for a fleeting moment. Then we come back and we talk. We tell each other what happened. We explore new territory and come back to report about it.

Until another silence occurs and we start it all over again.

Psychotherapy works best when it is connected with our experience. The difficulties of silence are one of many ways that we can have experiences in the therapy room that are then explored and integrated into your idea of who you are.

And finally, in silence, we are in our bodies, the bodies that didn't always speak. We are sitting with our cells which are older than language. And so in silence, we give more of ourselves an opportunity to come into the conversation. In using silence we deepen our experience, and thus we deepen our work. Carefully, gently, one little sliver at a time.

Talking with People In Your Life About Your Therapy

Guess what happened in therapy today?

Wouldn't you like to know? I sure as hell would like to tell you.

Then I wouldn't have to tell my therapist.

I sometimes think of therapy as a steam kettle – over time, the emotions rise. If I talk about what is happening for me in therapy with someone other than my therapist it is like taking the cover off the steam kettle. All the energy is released.

The problem is: this energy is the heart of the work. So if I release it outside the room, all that potential could go to waste.

For example, say that my therapist tells me that she is going away for two weeks in March.

I go home and I tell my partner "My therapist is going away. I can't believe she is going away again – she was away for three weeks over Christmas. It is like she is never here long enough for our work to deepen."

What have I done here? I let my anxiety and anger and upset bleed out of the therapy room. When I see my therapist again I am no longer as upset – I have expressed my feelings and been heard. But not by her. Something important has been said, but it has been said outside the room. As a result, the feelings that I have about her holiday are not expressed in the context of our relationship. Therefore I can't learn what the feelings mean. And I don't get the opportunity to experience my therapist's response to my feelings.

The urge to talk about therapy with friends and strangers is usually a way of managing our very strong feelings about what is happening in the room.

Some of us are eager to share. Some of us share nothing. Some of us share depending on the situation. However we are with talking, not talking, keeping secrets or being reticent –

whatever that brings up for us is meaningful. Therapy is a process of bringing our feelings to consciousness – of being aware of the choices we are making and how they feel. This allows us to explore ourselves a bit more deeply. There is a difference between keeping a secret and holding space for something in the place it belongs. This is an interesting distinction to explore over time while you are in therapy.

Talking about therapy can be very tempting. There can be a pull – sometimes salacious, sometimes furious, sometimes anxious – always filled with feelings. Most of us do it at one time or another. And that's OK. It isn't a moral question. This is a boundary that helps us grow. That helps us get the most out of the work.

When we bring our feelings to the person they concern, and when that person has the ability to listen deeply to us and respond, we have the possibility of moving from reflexive patterns to new discoveries. This is the edge of change.

Reflexive patterns are well-worn grooves, and thus often imperceptible. Holding up and creating a boundary that requires us to act differently requires considerable effort. But it is here, in this place of effort and discomfort, that the opportunity for something new emerges.

On the other hand – too much reticence may be a missed opportunity as well. At some point, therapy is worth talking about. Perhaps later on in the process when insights are digested and are no longer 'live' work. We need to talk about this work so that it is understood. This is my dream – that the brave and silent work that we do receives deeper understanding from a broader group of people. Psychotherapy has a particular and important voice to contribute to this world. Sometimes our shame keeps us quiet – this is worth exploring too.

I believe that in the right circumstance simply acknowledging that you see a therapist can be an important disclosure. A strong vulnerability that creates space for another's vulnerability.

And sometimes those outside conversations about therapy are really valuable for the therapy itself. As a therapist, I am grateful to the friends who encourage perseverance with the process or speak tenderly and supportively as my clients are in pain. Sharing is good. Your life is meant to be shared. If a person's only place where they share of themselves is therapy, I hold for them the possibility that loving relationships will bloom for them over time. The line between therapy and life is not even close to clear. In fact, I don't believe there really is a line.

So this is an ongoing puzzle. We each have our preference as to reticence versus disclosure. And in the particularity of our preference is the learning edge where deeper feelings come to the surface. Where we can share of ourselves. Where we can share what really matters to us. With our therapist and with the world.

Boundaries

Last night I thought of something I wish I had said to one of my clients.

I imagined emailing her.

And I thought about why I am not going to do that.

It would break the container.

What do I mean by the container?

Every week she comes to my office. I greet her in the waiting room and welcome her into my office. I close both sets of double doors behind her.

There we are safe. Sealed in.

She says what is on her mind.

I respond.

We work.

It is intimate. And sacred.

Set apart.

We can say things to each other because we are in a sealed room.

What we say to each other is not to be repeated outside the room.

The safety makes it possible for her to be a bit more vulnerable.

To tolerate a view of herself that hurts. Or say something she feels that she wouldn't dare say to someone in her life.

We are together moment by moment – reading each other's cues, examining what the experience is like for her.

I think of her after the session, but I don't email her.

Because email is not the sealed room.

Email is "every day" communication. Outside the container.

She and I have a contract that has to do with the sealed room.

That feeling we have of sitting down in the therapist's office for a different kind of conversation. A different experience.

It's this contract – or working alliance – that we have built over time that allows us to speak as we do – honestly.

We don't have to make each other feel better. We can speak the truth. And talk about how we feel about it.

We put the light of day on her and her life.

If I send an email "I was thinking about what we said and…."

She gets it in the midst of her daily life. She is not in therapy when she gets it. The communication is mixed in with many others. She may be with others when she gets it. She doesn't have a chance to respond. I can't see her face when she reads it.

It is outside the container that is therapy.

The baby on the plane is making eyes at me. She is thrilled with my smile. I am thrilled with hers. Her excitement overwhelms her, and she buries her face in her mother's shoulder.

She leans back on her mother's arm, looking at the ceiling and the lights. Then she looks to her mother and grabs her mother's lips with her hand. They look at each other.

Next, she is investigating the seat buckle. Grabbing at it. There is a latch that she catches on some of her grabs – she knows it is there, but she can't figure out how to get her hand to make it move.

She has a secure base – her mother is holding her. From here she explores the world. When she needs to come back to her mother – her mother is right there.

This is the container that we need in order to grow and explore and learn and thrive.

Therapy gives us a particular kind of holding that allows us to do new things we haven't done before. In the room, in each moment, we have the opportunity to turn back to the holding therapist for grounding. This holding is essential for the work of change.

There are many other types of containers.

Our first caregivers held us.

Our homes hold us.

Our pets hold us.

Nature holds us.

People hold us.

We can grow into an ability to hold ourselves. Or to allow our physical environment to hold us.

Often, we need a person to hold us for a good long while before we can do this. A lot depends on how we were handed over to ourselves in our original holding.

The container is not a concept – it is an experience.

If I email my client in this instance, it would be a poke rather than a holding.

We know we are held when we can let ourselves exhale and be the people we are.

The end of the session

A lot can happen at the end of a session.

How does your therapist end the session? How do you feel about it? Or do you end the session?

Important things are often said right at the end of a session.

Therapists call these important things that are said while a client is leaving "doorknob moments".

It is the time when you might make a joke that shows your true feelings.

Or bring up a topic on your mind that you don't want to talk about so you mention it just at the last moment when there is no time to discuss it.

Or a topic that you do want to explore. Doing this is frustrating for you and your therapist. Is this a repetition of a pattern for you in some way? Not letting yourself have the thing that you need?

Like all aspects of the frame around therapy it can be fruitful to be observant about how your sessions end. Bring your thoughts and feelings to the next session to talk about when there is plenty of time.

Endings can be difficult. They represent our first frustrations and our most recent losses.

Endings are great therapeutic material.

CHAPTER 4
DIGGING IN

Cultivating Change

We often use the word 'work' when we talk about therapy.

Doing inner work. Doing our work. Working on our problems.

There is a level of effort required.

Therapy is a practice that unfolds over time.

We need to go to our sessions. Regularly.

We need to try to say what is on our mind. To consider our therapist's response. To take risks.

Maybe small ones. And we do need to push ourselves. A bit. Put in the work.

STARTING THERAPY

But working too hard doubles back on itself. If we work too hard we are telling ourselves: 'you aren't alright just as you are. You need to try harder.'

This is a self-defeating message.

You might say – no, it's not. I definitely have such and such a problem, and it needs to be fixed.

This might very well be true. It might be true that you hope for something from therapy. But you need to hold yourself with kindness. To take in some of your therapist's stance towards you and care and attend to yourself with understanding that you are how you are for a very good reason. And that you, as you are, are exactly enough.

Pushing too hard will get in the way of the work. The tender and vulnerable parts of you that need to come out – those parts won't respond to pushing.

My meditation teacher once said, "Sit on the forward edge of your cushion."

What she meant is this: try, but don't try. This is of course a paradox.

This is the fruitful edge of the "work."

Sometimes the work is cultivating that edge. The edge that will enable us to grow and change.

This is relevant to many things that we want but can not fully control if, how and when they happen. Falling in love, getting a job, building a business, having a family, living a long life. Our lives are all subject to the circumstances, experiences and interactions that they are filled with.

What can you do to nurture this energy that you are looking to grow in your life?

All we can do is cultivate. Create the necessary conditions.

We can't make any of these things happen.

So our work is nesting, cultivating, creating containers.

How do we do this?

We notice our dreams and acknowledge the energies that we see.

We draw, sculpt, imagine, write.

We garden, make our homes beautiful, exercise our bodies.

We meditate. We speak our dreams and fantasies. And we particularly do this in therapy.

We speak what is on our mind without censorship in a held space where our words can be examined.

This is another way of working hard. Building a nest at the edge between conscious and unconscious.

STARTING THERAPY

How Therapy Helps Us Change

Sometimes a savvy new client will say something along the lines of "I know that understanding by itself won't bring about change – I don't just want to dredge up the past for nothing."

These words could mean a lot of different things. That meaning is of course particular to each person.

When clients say this, I hear two things in particular.

(1) I don't just want to talk – I want lasting change.
(2) I am afraid of the pain that is lurking beneath the surface, and I am afraid to feel that pain.

Some people come to therapy having never talked with another person about themselves. In therapy, they learn to formulate an expression of their experience. The words become an articulation that in itself helps them to understand. For example, "I was hurt when my mother did X." For them, these expressions are entirely new and as such are agents of change. By having the thought, expressing it, and having it met with an empathic response, the world of the client changes bit by bit.

Clients who come in already "knowing the causes of their problems" are rightly resistant to going over this material again. It isn't new. So it is just talking. For this client to say, "I was hurt when my mother did X" doesn't get them any further than telling me, "I graduated from UWO in 1993."

What we're after is not understanding but experience. With the first client, it looks like they are gaining understanding. And this is certainly a side benefit of much therapeutic work. But what they are really having is an experience. An experience of having a feeling, putting it into words and having it received by another person. And this is what the more self-aware client also needs. But not about the "old stuff." They need to begin to articulate "new stuff."

So how does this happen? It happens when you, the client, commit to speaking in detail and often about everything that is happening for you. I don't mean telling endless stories "about things." I mean speaking about your experience – your experience in the world and your experience in the therapy room. Your thoughts, feelings, fantasies, dreams, curiosities… you need to bring yourself to the room. All those parts that you often leave behind when you face the world.

This can be the things that seem as "little" as your irritation at the dumb magazines in the waiting room, or the "silly" butterflies you feel in your stomach when you look in the mirror. You don't need to understand the meaning, either. You don't even need to try to understand the meaning. Just bring yourself.

Together, you and your therapist follow the trails of your experience. In doing this you are following the breadcrumbs that help you to find who and what you need to find.

We don't know what is at the end of the path. By definition we do not know. But we know there is a path. And if we can follow the path with faith our work will bear fruit.

Another word for faith might be "working alliance." A working alliance is a good relationship between you and your therapist – you know you are on the same team. You are on the case together.

When you follow the breadcrumbs of your inner self, you will encounter pain. And it will be difficult. But it will not be for naught. Together you and your therapist will approach it directly in a new way because you and her on that day you approach it – you are new – never the same as you were before. And if you stay with your experience on that day and you work together who knows what you will find?

Or, more accurately, who knows what changes will happen?

Taking in something new

It sometimes irks me when people talk about "retail therapy." Shopping is not the same as psychotherapy. It feels to me like they are reducing the work of psychotherapy to a fling or an addiction. A quick fix. Something that can be purchased.

I have given this term some thought, however, and have come to understand it a little more.

Retail therapy is not just shopping. It is when we go shopping because we are sad, upset, afraid, nervous, or in some other way distraught. The act of choosing new things and buying them for ourselves is supposed to make us feel better.

I recognize this behaviour in myself. Mostly it comes out in ordering books from Amazon when I am having a bad day. If I examine the feeling closely I come to this: the desire to have something new. It is not only the thing itself that I want. With Amazon I have to wait at least a day to get it anyway. It is the satisfaction of seeing the order confirmation in my inbox. And then when the box arrives – more satisfaction. But if I'm honest, the percentage of books that get read (i.e. used) is very low. The wanting and getting and owning is what is important.

That's retail therapy. A search for satisfaction that ends up at the local thrift store in next year's spring cleaning.

One of the ways I think therapy works is that we are taking in something new. We take in new ideas.

We also take in our therapist's orientation to the world – in their tone, choice of words, concepts, reactions, and movements. We absorb their responses to us. We start to comprehend something different than we had before.

Here is an example:

Client: I could never quit school – my parents would kill me.

Therapist: Because?

Client: Because they could never have a quitter in the family.

The client makes a statement. I imagine that the therapist feels a response – they are slightly unsettled – they don't understand the connection between quitting school and the parents' disapproval. The therapist can imagine the connection from their own experience, but they don't know the truth for this particular client. It is not a given to the therapist that parents 'kill' their kids for quitting school. And thus they ask for clarification.

The client pauses and then explains the family's strong aversion to quitting. In that pause, the client has digested a sliver of what the therapist was feeling – that there is not a necessary connection between quitting and parental rage and disapproval. It might be brief, but it's there.

And so this is the similarity I see to "retail therapy." The taking in of something new. But unlike the book that goes unread – what you take in in therapy is experiential. You cannot help but use it because it is something you have taken inside yourself. Before you even realize it you've used it. You can reject it – which is another way of using it.

I think this is why people often leave therapy abruptly. The taking in was too much. The internal experience is overwhelming and they don't know what to do with it and since they don't know what is happening they quickly cut off the source of the feeling. They are unconsciously saying "this must not be good." While consciously saying, "my therapist doesn't really get me," or "I don't really need this."

And you can see from the example that this isn't about the therapist going on a long diatribe with their opinions and the client agreeing or disagreeing with their thoughts. The taking in happens in micro moments. Moments that are experienced by both client and therapist. Moments that happen before we put words to them.

This is another way in which therapy is much more than "talk" or "dredging up the past." We are actually, physically, experientially, taking something in. We are acquiring new things. We want some kind of change, and we go out to find it. Retail therapy for the soul.

The relationship between self care and therapy

Take care of yourself.

When we think of self-care we tend to think of indulgence. We might think of the spa. But then we think about it. "I can do that later." "Too expensive." "I have too much to do." "There are more important things to be done."

Actually, resourcing yourself is the most important thing you do. The *most* important.

It doesn't matter what else has to be done. If you are not available to the task in front of you, you are a less than whole person in the action you are doing.

We're all half-people sometimes.

But if we want to connect ourselves to our lives we have to rest. We have to be nourished. We have to listen to our needs. The needs of our body, mind, and soul.

We have limits – that is what it is to be a human being. But so often we act like we do not. We're told that we can be anything. Do everything. That we have infinite possibilities.

But – when we don't respect and nurture the body container in which we live we undo our possibilities.

When we resource ourselves, rest, set boundaries, and rejuvenate – then we allow our work in the world to unfold.

By work I mean love. Care. Creativity.

The more closely I pay attention to this in myself and others the more it is clear to me that this is one of the deepest issues we face.

We are up against ourselves and our self-concept in our moment-by-moment choices about how to be in the world. And I do mean moment-by-moment.

It's quite convenient. We don't take care of ourselves. So we're not available enough to feel into what is actually happening around us. And thus we can't do anything about it. It's a get out clause. An excuse.

Who benefits from this?

Reflect on what this is a repetition of.

The work of change and healing for ourselves and the world is the work of moment-by-moment decisions that allow our tender and strong hearts space to live and be and express themselves.

This is the hardest work. And it has very little to do with the spa.

Poetic Aside: What it feels like to change[4]

We tend to think that change happens like magic – a switch flips and we are in love, rich, or no longer anxious. We fantasize about vacations of bliss. And when we arrive there is bliss and a sunburn and a frozen drink too many and, well, real life in all its glory.

Deep change involves bearing a process which we do not yet understand. It involves changing from one physical, emotional, and intellectual organism into another. It does not happen all at once but in increments, all the time, whether we want to or not. Our existence in interaction with life is constantly changing.

Even when change is something that we want, when change is something that we intentionally seek out, we still have to bear it. We have to accept it when it happens and when it doesn't. We have to handle the shape it takes. We have to take its speed – fast, slow, or something in between.

---

[4] A version of this article first appeared on Elephant Journal.

STARTING THERAPY

Change is an interaction with something new. Over time, I have come to recognize change as it is happening. At least sometimes.

Sometimes my brain goes fuzzy or suddenly empty.

Sometimes I feel depleted. And thirsty. Like my psyche just had an intense massage.

Sometimes I feel jacked up and manic.

Sometimes I feel butterflies.

Sometimes my shame is activated and past regrets, mistakes, and vulnerabilities take over with an insatiable vengeance.

Sometimes someone says something unexpected, and I consciously try to take it in. To let it change my cells.

Sometimes I cry about something I have never cried about before.

Sometimes I have a dream or fantasy, and part of its meaning hits home and I know that this is a marker of an incremental shift.

Sometimes someone in my life puts words to a change and I recognize it as true but previously unarticulated. In talking, the change takes shape. It is given physical form.

Sometimes I have an extra glass of wine that I don't need or even want. Later, I can identify this extra glass as a response to new feelings that seemed unmanageable even though unworded.

Some of these changes are about my conscious self. Some are about unconscious aspects that I cannot fully articulate.

And sometimes there is no perceptible sign of anything.

When we seek out the new, we change in response.

Thinking

Something that therapy develops in particular: thinking.

In therapy, thinking is at issue.

Your therapist wants to know all of your thoughts. Whatever is on your mind. However it is on your mind.

Scattered, confused, focussed – it's all relevant.

The therapist listens to what is on your mind and responds.

So you get some feedback on your thinking.

But not just any feedback. Careful and considered feedback. Each response from the therapist is created in the moment with the intention of helping you and them to understand you. (There might be other intentions, too, but that's a major one).

Together, you come to understand how you understand the world. The meanings you make of it.

STARTING THERAPY

And then – this is so important – you have the experience of thinking alongside another person.

We all know the person who is on an endless loop with the thoughts in their own head. Who talks as if you aren't there. Conversation happens when we can say what is in our own head and then listen to the response and allow it to take us outside of where we were.

Our thinking is developed by being thought with.

Not told how to think but another person trying to understand your thinking in particular.

Thinking in relationship is a way of connecting.

It also changes us. As our thinking evolves so does our life. That is why the topic of thinking is so important.

I remember moments of elation early in therapy where I realized I could say what I was saying and my therapist was listening – often enjoying – my thoughts, observations, realizations. She took me seriously. I think she even learned some things from me. We were in conversation.

Nowadays, as you can tell, my thinking is very important to me. Crucial, really. And despite a decent formal education, I have developed my ability to think and articulate my thinking primarily through psychotherapy.

But thinking gets a bad reputation sometimes.

Psychodynamic therapists often dismiss cognitive therapy as not going deep enough, or dealing "only with thoughts."

Some forms of meditation have us watch our thoughts as just thoughts, without attention or care for the content.

Intellectualization is sometimes seen as a defence, or a criticism that you are too "in your head."

"Overthinking" is often considered a negative trait.

While there is some truth to all of these statements, I think the reality is much deeper than this.

Our thoughts are part of us. In us. They come from our embodied selves.

They're as important as anything else. And yet can't be seen as entities on their own without our bodies and souls.

This is where we can get into trouble – when we don't see our thinking as a thing in itself but rather see the content of our thinking as a true definition of the world.

In therapy, thinking – the content and the act of – are both the issue at hand.

Facts

Being a therapist involves entering into many worlds in one day.

Each client brings a world. A world of people, activities, feelings, and beliefs.

For many people their beliefs are facts. The work of therapy is often to realize that facts are just beliefs. It is a softening, a widening of vision. It is an understanding of our context, of how that context shifts, and then of our possibility within that context.

Facts don't offer much possibility. They are definite, known, proven and true.

Except when they're not.

Examples of facts that are actually beliefs include:

Parents pay for the wedding.

Men don't cry.

Women talk a lot.

I will have children.

Everything is fine.

Facts bind us tightly. When life challenges them, we hold fast. As the evidence mounts against one of our favourite "facts" we need more and more energy to hold on to them. Even if we know that they might be wrong And thus we are tired.

When we are tired we are not at our best.

Our dreams scream.

We have an extra beer or two just to numb the pain.

We are grumpy with the people we love for no reason.

We eat a lot of cheese pizza that we don't really want.

The storm might pass on its own.

Or we may be forced to reexamine the facts.

If we decide to enter therapy we start out by telling our therapist all of these facts.

It usually feels amazing to pour it all out. The whole scenario from our point of view. To someone who is on our side.

And then a few sessions in something our therapist says irritates us. Or perhaps it just seems so wrong we interrupt her to explain why what she is implying is not at all the case. That she simply does not understand.

Or perhaps she asks a question that we hear as an interpretation that we must reject. So we do so at great length. Vigorously.

Or we hear her question and we cry. Because no one has ever realized this before. We know in our core she is right. And finally we have let it out.

This is the work of examining the facts.

The world itself changes. It changes into an infinite number of facts that are not facts. A constantly changing place that cannot be pinned down or explained in any comprehensive way.

Done for long enough, a sustained practice over time in the therapy room and your world changes.

The Weight Of Our Thoughts

If you and I are meeting for coffee on Friday, I will think of you during the week. From time to time the thought of you will come into my mind. I will think of the last time we spoke, the topics that might come up and questions I would like to ask you. I will imagine our conversation. I will imagine the place and the drink and/or snack I might have.

Depending on our relationship I will have various feelings about our upcoming meeting. I may feel nervous or excited. The reasons for our meeting will affect how I feel. I might have some news or I may need you for something. I may be concerned about you or afraid of what you might have to say to me. All of our history together and all of my history on this planet impact my orientation towards you on Friday.

None of this is conscious. It is not a formal process. It consists of brief flashes, moments, memories, logistical plans. The thought of our coffee just flits through my brain like the wind. And one moment later I am thinking of something else. But it's happening. As events draw closer, they take up more brain space – or I might say body space.

And so my preparation for you is inevitable.

When we meet, we don't meet blank. We're never blank.

From how I'm feeling to what happened last night, I come loaded. As do you.

My ideas about you and how this experience will be are dense and thick – and probably largely off the mark.

And then we have our experience.

It's a wonder we can experience anything new at all, with all of this in our heads already.

And often we don't. Conversations can be more like side by side presentations – two people but no exchange. Or the performance of a scenario that we have rehearsed repeatedly in our minds.

Sometimes in therapy we try to unpack this loadedness that we bring to our sessions. We talk about what we imagined talking about. Our feelings, thoughts, glimmers throughout the week. These reveal much about our orientation, our being, and our history. Especially when our expectation upon arrival turns out to be different from what we encounter when we are actually in session.

We imagine getting angry at our therapist and instead talk around a knotty problem for a while.

We imagine telling our therapist how much they mean to us and instead tell a dream.

We come with thoughts and ideas and feelings, and when we get to therapy, we go somewhere else entirely.

We arrive feeling we were too much in the last session; too much. And on voicing it we find out that this was not at all our therapist's experience. That she welcomes that part of us.

We come feeling good, thinking we're fine now, and it is about time to end this therapy. And we leave having uncovered another layer that we now want to explore.

And on and on.

Among many other things, therapy is an awareness practice. A practice of doing something that opens us up, increases our understanding, broadens our experience, and helps us to strengthen our muscles and open ourselves wider to try new things outside the room.

The weight of my imagination often tires me. I am glad for the many hours of talking in therapy that has morphed it into a more engaging and responsive creature.

Feeling

We tend to be more comfortable with some feelings than with others. Some feel easier to deal with. And we have our default ways of expressing ourselves.

If we are a crier, it can cover over anger.

If we are angry, it can cover over tears.

The full range of emotions – sadness, joy, anger, envy, fear – feeling all of these is part of exploring yourself in therapy.

Notice when you have a resistance to a particular feeling as if it is not allowed or not safe to express. These are the ways we have learned to rein ourselves in and bury our emotions. The full expression of these feelings will most likely be a profound experience of release.

I'm Sorry For Crying

"I'm sorry for crying. I'll try not to next time."

Over and over again I hear this as a therapist.

It is one of those things that breaks my heart.

I want to say lean forward and say, "Cry. Cry. And then cry some more. There is so much to cry about. Let it out. Let yourself be sad and undone."

It is a moment when sometimes a client is full of emotion and unable to take in my openness. They are sure I don't want them to cry.

And they are keeping that part of themselves – the part that grieves – in line. In check. Held back.

It doesn't have to make sense.

It doesn't have to be justified.

Some people long to be able to shed tears.

When tears come they are a gift.

There's nothing selfish about letting yourself cry.

Crying shows us what matters to us. It expresses a part of who we are.

Every time I cry in the presence of someone else they say to me, "Just let it out. Don't hold it in."

The consistency of this response has made it clear to me that I do also hold in my tears. And that sometimes I want to.

I don't apologize anymore.

At other times I want to cry. But I can't. I can't access the tears. I can try to let it out, but they don't often flow.

When tears come they are a gift.

Sadness sits in us and creates a pressure that needs to be released and shared.

Being sad isn't popular.

It isn't transcendent.

Or positive.

Or is it?

What would it be like if we let ourselves cry?

No explaining. No advice. Just tears.

Tears shed and tears shared.

Perhaps it would be human.

The Unconscious

You wouldn't be coming to therapy if you knew everything.

Keep that in mind.

You don't tell your heart to beat. You don't tell your stomach to digest your food. You don't tell yourself to breathe. You just breathe. These and many other body systems are unconscious.

You can, however, breathe at will. And you can increase your heart rate through exercise and decrease it through rest. These are some of the ways you can consciously impact your physical processes.

We are a combination of conscious and unconscious processes.

Your conscious self – the self you know every day – has to bring you to therapy. It makes the decision, makes the appointment, walks into the office. But they bring with them all of you – including the parts of you which you are not consciously directing such as your beating heart and your digesting stomach.

You have probably experienced the less conscious parts of yourself in other ways, too. In a pattern that you keep repeating despite knowing that it is not good for you. Or in something you say that just "slips" out the "wrong" way.

That is why it is scary to start a new relationship, and that is why it is scary to start therapy. Because you might see something you haven't seen before. Because you might experience something you haven't experienced before.

And that's why you're here.

You're not here to stay the same.

If you understand the challenge of bringing yourself into this new situation, if you can be aware from the beginning that not every part of you feels the same way about this venture. This will help you.

Be aware that there are parts of you that you do not understand and that getting to know these parts will serve you well in this project, despite how difficult it may be to do so.

Dreams

You may find that your therapist is interested in your dreams. I hope you will also come to be interested in your dreams.

You create your dreams. Not your conscious part that has a lot to say, a lot of opinions, and a lot to do. Your conscious part that is often a censor.

No – your dreams are created when the busy conscious part is asleep. This is amazing. Your dreams are expressions of your self – the part of you that you do not have regular and straightforward access to.

Dreams are messages as much as your conscious thoughts and feelings are messages.

Dream analysis is complex. There is no one right way to interpret dreams just as there is no one right way to interpret a person.

But if you follow your dreams you will be amazed at what you find there.

What is true of dreams is also true of daydreams, fantasies, jokes, and slips. Anything that you say or do without inhibition is gold. It is gold because it expresses something of your true situation or feelings. This may be different from the way you think about yourself and the world. Your unconscious may have other ideas than those you hold consciously.

Some people become perturbed at the idea of having unconscious parts of themselves. It is very important that each of us has unconscious parts. It is important that you breathe and digest and that your heart beats without you doing anything consciously. It is important that you can't feel all your feelings all the time. Having an unconscious is crucial to life.

And it is alright that you have feelings and thoughts that contradict themselves and some of which you don't want to admit to anyone, ever, even yourself. This is human. This is life. Therapy is partly about coming to understand yourself as human in this way.

And so it is alright if it takes you a while to get used to this idea.

Notice how you say things, even when you think what you have said is "wrong". Notice your first reactions. Notice your fantasies – grandiose and embarrassing as they may be. I have grown to trust my fantasies through this work and they are a source of creativity and sustenance inside and outside the room.

Your fantasies too have a lot to offer.

Some practical notes on dreams:

If you want to remember your dream and you do not usually remember them, state your intention or desire before you go to bed. It can be as simple as, "I would like to remember a dream tomorrow morning." Say it out loud to yourself.

Write down or dictate your dreams into your phone before you get out of bed. You will catch the most detail at this time. You will also catch yourself in that semi-conscious state which allows you to see an expanded view of what you are thinking and feeling, before the critic and editor has woken up.

Dreams are private things. What appears to be "nonsense" can express deep feelings and meanings. Of all my writing I keep dreams the most private. We have to be free to dream and to write them down freely. I also rarely tell people my dreams. I share only with those I deeply trust.

Work with your dreams. Read them, mull them over, associate to them. By this I mean say or write what comes to mind when you think of the various elements. What do you think of when you think of an elephant? Draw them. Buy symbols. I remember a dream long ago of wearing a duck suit. I bought a duck nose and wore it around the house. I inhabited the feeling of my dream. This may sound ridiculous That's the point. Our unconscious makes a sense that is all its own. By respecting that sense and believing in it even when we don't have a clue about its rational meaning we encourage its expression. As we inhabit our dreams they bear fruit.

Projection

Suppose you are working in a group of people. You have a common project.

You start to feel like you are not doing a good job. The group, you imagine, thinks you are not pulling your weight. They think you are not skilled at what you are doing. Or not knowledgeable.

As a result perhaps you work harder – trying to please – sacrificing your time and effort for the project.

Your frustration and upset mounts. This is not an enjoyable experience.

Perhaps you grow resentful and make cranky remarks.

Perhaps you become critical of the group and tell your friend all about how you don't like what they are doing. While in group meetings you are flat and uninterested.

Then one day someone says, "Thank-you – that was very helpful when you sent out that email with an update." And another group member agrees, "Yes – that really contributed."

So now you see that your contribution is valued. That the lack of information about your value left room for you to make up your own story.

So what was happening? Your feeling about the situation was one thing. The reality was another.

And your actions were based on this unreality. You made choices based on something that wasn't true.

Let's go one step further.

Why did you think you weren't valuable to the group? Where did you get that idea?

Well – you came up with it. It was your idea.

Your own view of yourself was projected onto the group.

You believe at some level that you are not good at what you do. That you are not valuable as a person.

And so you assume the group feels that way.

Which infuriates, hurts, upsets, agitates you. And you respond.

And what do you think the group does? Get frustrated with you.

And thus your views are confirmed. It's a cycle. A vicious one.

But in the scenario above, the group valued you and your actions. Your reaction to your own views and your projection of them did not annoy the group too badly. They showed appreciation for what you brought to the team.

You took your inward views of yourself, your inward experience of yourself and you put it out (unconsciously) into the world.

We all do this all of the time.

We can't feel directly our feelings about ourselves – it would upset us too much. But we must live in the world ordered as we know it to be ordered, and so we put the feelings out in the world.

When we see someone for who they are we are connected to them. The same happens with ourself – when we see ourselves for who we are we know ourselves and are more fully alive and connected to our deepest selves.

Our projection is a leaping away from ourselves.

Self-love is not a nebulous or illusory proposition.

Self-love is the exploring of oneself. It's the staying with oneself. Just like we do with a loved one who needs us.

Without self-love we live in the world through the lens of self-hatred.

And then look what happens.

To our planet.

To each other.

To our leaders.

No matter how egregious the personal or political horror or insult we must do our own work.

We must ground ourselves in ourselves. Be absorbed in ourselves. Work with the projection.

We must struggle with the fact that the conflict might be inside of us. We must struggle with this first. Consider it. Question it.

We must try to clear ourselves from the brambles of ourselves. It is the trying that is important because it sets us in a direction.

So that then we can speak.

So that then we can act.

So that then we can stay the course.

This all starts with expressing our feelings in the client's chair and considering what they might mean. This all starts with not believing everything we say to ourselves.

Your relationship with your therapist

> "If you have come here to help me, you are wasting your time. But if you have come because your liberation is bound up with mine, then let us work together."
>
> –Lilla Watson

The relationship between therapist and client is the container for everything that happens in therapy.

Following on from the previous section on projection, the thoughts and feelings you have about your therapist and the thoughts and feelings your therapist have about you are part of the process of therapy.

In school we are often trained to learn from the teacher.

With a therapist you are both co-creating in every moment.

STARTING THERAPY

Therapy can be a shelter in the storm of life – a place where you can say anything and where you know you will be listened to and helped.

Therapy can be a place to explore how you relate. From the beginning of the session, in everything that you do and say in your particular way, you are building and establishing a connection. Your therapist experiences you and how you do this, and can talk with you about you.

Therapy can be a place to have a new relational experience: curiosity, compassion, humour, intelligence, challenge, fury, cherishing.

It is a place to discover things in relationship that you didn't know could be there. This is why it takes a long time to do some kinds of work. Because you don't even know what is possible and you can't hear it, let alone experience it. Until one day you do.

And your therapist is there holding a part of you. Being with you in a way that you just didn't think could happen.

Therapy can be a place where you take in someone else's view. Sometimes I say to clients, "if you can't speak to yourself compassionately ask yourself what I would say about you in that moment." They know what I would say and thus a part of them knows how to be compassionate to themselves. They just have to find that part in me rather than themselves. For now.

Psychotherapy follows the client. It is a relationship based on the well-being and healing of the client. This can be a very new experience for some. Whether at home, school, or work most of us are used to people needing things from us. A relationship where your well-being is the first priority can feel unnatural. Most of us are also used to a doctor – patient model where the "expert" offers the "cure." Psychotherapy works on a different model. Together, you and your therapist work towards helping you understand yourself. Because this is not how most treatments in our culture work it can be very disorienting at first. This disorientation is part of the work of helping you reconnect to yourself.

The ability to talk about anything, confidentially, and with an eye to growth and healing, is a unique feature of therapy.

If we are open, we can find the unexpected, the new, and maybe even what it is that we seek – in each other.

Wondering about your therapist

Who is this person you are pouring yourself out to?

Some clients are curious about their therapist. Others don't want to know a thing.

Your therapist may choose to answer your questions or they may not. Therapists have different ways of disclosing about themselves.

But however much your therapist shares, your questions are important. Ask away. What are you curious about? What do you perceive? How do you imagine your therapist's life outside the room? Do you hope to or fear running into your therapist outside of the therapy office? All of this is worth exploration.

About your therapist

Your therapist is paying attention to you and the relationship moment by moment. Her training has involved getting to know her own reactions and becoming used to attuning to others.

When her mind wanders, she is trained to notice where it wanders to – this is information. When she has a daydream or fantasy during sessions she notices this. She notices her physical sensations, her thoughts, and her feelings in relationship to you. All of this is information that she can use to understand you and then help you.

If you say something that upsets your therapist or she doesn't know what to do about a situation, she has colleagues and supervisors who work with her to help her make sense of what is happening. There is a structure in the profession that supports each other. Supervisors are senior therapists – therapists in private practice can usually choose their supervisors and they pay them by the hour for supervision. Therapists are not employees of their supervisors.

Supervision is done confidentially. Usually, only first names are used. The relationship follows the same ethics as that of therapist-client. Your therapist's supervisor considers your therapist's relationship with you and helps her to understand what is happening between you.

Being a therapist is creative and daunting work. I regularly feel that I do not know what I am doing. This is good – it means I am opening myself up to possibility. I am trying to take in the worlds of my patients.

But we are also well trained. To handle you and ourselves. A good therapist is always working. A good therapist does the work for themselves and for you.

Does your therapist understand you?

Your therapist understands some things about you. There are other things they just don't get.

This is perfect. And normal. Because you are in a relationship.

What is important in this relationship is the process of understanding. Of coming to understand each other.

As Donna Orange writes,

> My patient who seems to have everything, including everything that I have never had, but continues to return to a truly abusive partner, one who throws hot soup on her in anger and rages at her in front of friends and family confounds me. Then I remember that understanding is a difficult practice and that there is

clearly something we have not understood together yet.[5]

Sometimes we want to be understood without having to speak our needs. Like a child, we think we should just be met and immediately absorbed.

When someone can do this for us it is a gift.

But even better is the gift that two people receive when they continue to be present to one other even when they don't understand everything. When they commit to each other despite difference and despite distance. The difficult practice of understanding is worth the uphill trek. To be understood in a way that you haven't been before is the bedrock of change.

My therapist often does not understand me.

I am glad for that (most days) because finding each other is sweet.

I have a crush on my therapist

Usually, there is a fair bit of distress around this topic. Not knowing how to deal with the feelings. And wondering if they are appropriate.

My thinking (influenced by many writers and colleagues) goes something like this:

---

[5] *The Suffering Stranger: Hermeneutics for Everyday Clinical Practice*, Routledge, Donna Orange, 2011.

We are born seeking satisfaction. The satisfaction of milk, of urinating and defecating, of seeing something new and taking it in, of being held.

The seeking of satisfaction is experienced as excitement. An upswing in nervous system energy.

When or if this seeking of satisfaction is related to genital activity we call it sexual.

The energy towards satisfaction is common to sexual and non-sexual endeavours: the eagerness to raise your hand and comment/question, the desire to reach out and hold, the excitement to bite into or sip.

In this context, a crush on your therapist is one of many possible excitements in an adult life.

Other examples that come to mind: the book or film we can't stop reading or talking about. The new project or idea that occupies our mind. The new friendship or travel destination that captures us.

And in fact, excitement happens all day long. I pause for a moment in my chair to think about what I am writing. And then thoughts come and I feel my body pick up the pace and my fingers rush for the keyboard and they move quickly as I type, trying to get the thoughts down, excited by what has come. And then another pause. A satisfaction – small but present. And then more thinking and then – oh – I am excited again and have more words for you. The closer I stay to my physical experience, the more interesting this gets.

In the context of therapy, a crush could be a reawakening of a long dormant wanting. Perhaps for romantic love and sexual passion. But perhaps also a long dormant need to be seen and cherished – to be the apple of someone's eye. Whether that was your childhood experience or not, the experience of therapy can awaken these desires in a powerful way.

Our excitements will often have their roots in deep feeling. What is happening is precious creativity, an expression of vitality – your being is offering you a chance to expand. These surprising excitements bear great fruit when they are welcomed and articulated into being. The fear associated with going there is part of the excitement and part of the discovery.

The boundaries of a therapeutic relationship are the perfect place to see what unfolds from this kind of exploration. To see what deep voice is speaking and what new satisfaction it is seeking.

All excitements in and out of therapy are worth this kind of noticing and respect. Maturation is the process of being able to bear in our nervous systems and our souls the unfurling of an excitement, a sensation. With no immediate satisfaction. And seeing where it takes us.

So yes – it is a rich and appropriate gift to have a crush on your therapist. Talking about this will be an exploration that could leave a deep imprint on you and your work in therapy.

Our Development

Each of us comes into the world differently. We are unique. And the environment we come into is unique. It is a therapy cliché that therapists want to hear about problems with parents. Clients rightly reject this idea. Therapists are not looking to blame or critique. They are, however, very interested in *your experience*.

For example, A very outgoing child raised by two shy and insecure parents may have received all the love in the world. And they may grow up with a sense of having had nowhere to put their energy and desire for connection. They may be starving for connection. Or shut down completely. They will have some kind of response to their parents.

All of us do. We are products of how things have been for us throughout our lifetime. Our first few years are particularly important. These are the years when our bodies absorb everything. These are the years when we learn how to be in the world. Not do but be. We learn we are safe (or not), that our needs matter to those around us (or not). We learn how people respond to us when we do different things. We learn the language of interacting in a physical way.

As therapy progresses you get down to the heart of the matter. The deepest pains, insecurities and tensions that come up for you. A developmental perspective is often helpful here.

A client says to me about a current situation, "I don't know if I will make it out of this."

And I wonder if she felt that when she was young and her alcoholic father was in a rage. She probably did. And so her adult life challenges take on an extra urgency. They are life or death. This is the accurate emotional accounting she did when she was three, and it persists to this day.

When we can connect to our own experience as we were vulnerable and growing quickly and taking it all in we can understand ourselves. Why certain things are such "big deals". Why we have trouble getting over certain things.

The developmental perspective is easy to dismiss. I think we often dismiss it because the feelings are so huge. Sometimes we can't connect to them. Sometimes we don't want to. We fear altering our relationships and our memories.

Keep at it and keep an open mind. Our lived experience is all we have. It's what we bring to the table. And it begins early when our understanding of things is still very much in process. At this time, things that appear small to adults can have huge impacts.

Difficulties in therapy

Therapy is usually a pretty bumpy road.

Undergoing change means that the equilibrium you have set up in your life will shift. It has to shift to facilitate the change.

You may have a breakthrough and then regress back to bad habits and depressed feelings a few days later.

People may be upset by the changes that happen as a result of your work in therapy.

This is all part of the work.

Expecting difficulty might help prepare you for this.

If the work of therapy is to unearth what you don't understand then the work of therapy will be difficult and it will feel unfamiliar. We push away what we do not want to think and feel. There is a reason we do this. Even if we are not aware of it. To figure ourselves out requires releasing some of this buried material.

Everyone's difficulties will look different, but I am confident that you will encounter some.

Two common difficulties that often arise are time and money.

Soon after beginning therapy, you may find that you start missing appointments.

Your schedule just doesn't let you get there some weeks. Money is tight. You are not sure if you and your therapist are really a fit.

This is a very important stage.

It feels from the inside like it is about time and money.

It is rarely about time and money.

STARTING THERAPY

It is about how you are sorting through the various commitments in your life. It is about the relative value you are placing on therapy.

You are reducing the relative value you are placing on therapy because something is happening that you don't like.

If you go to your session you know you will hear something you don't like, have to face something you don't want to face. Almost imperceptibly our beings rearrange the logistics of our lives to suit our emotional stance.

Ask yourself why you don't want to go. Take a moment and let those feelings be there. Notice the impulse to relegate therapy to secondary importance.

And remember why you are going in the first place.

Remember that the process takes time.

And then – if you can – keep your regular appointment and bring these feelings to therapy.

For therapy to be effective, you must go to your appointments.

You must work regularly.

The urge to put off therapy until next week is a sign that things are happening. Uncomfortable things perhaps, but things that are pushing you to a new place. Remember, we go to therapy to change.

Bearing Uncertainty is Hard Work

So often clients want takeaways from their sessions. Advice, suggestions, insights…

I understand. I want these things too.

We want progress.

The type of therapy I practice usually involves great gains in the first ten sessions.

It's an opportunity to be heard. To express feelings you can't always express.

Often there are big insights and connections.

And often, after about ten sessions (and that is a huge generalization), the "progress" slows.

What do I mean by this? I mean the feeling that after every session we "got somewhere."

This can be really frustrating. And disorienting.

Why come to a session if you don't get anywhere? What is the point of talking about all this stuff?

Here's the reframe:

If we come to therapy wanting to shift something… relationship patterns, a sense of meaning, depression…

If we come to therapy wanting to shift something there is something we don't understand. Our being is not transparent to us. That's the current situation.

It's a big situation. It's your whole self over your whole life coming to this place to figure something out that is of utmost importance to you.

There is no way it can all be figured out in an hour. Or ten hours.

The process of deep change in psychotherapy requires that we hold a certain degree of uncertainty.

It requires that we hold a certain degree of not understanding.

The first step is often to make this lack of understanding explicit.

"This is a mystery."

"I wonder what is happening here?"

We have to lay out the mystery – all the pieces. It takes time.

It's hour by hour work.

Bearing the fact that we don't understand something is an acknowledgment of our complexity.

A complex problem takes time.

Our culture doesn't support this place well.

We need to have updates, opinions, actions.

We need to get value for money.

We need to buy things.

But what if right now you just don't know the answer?

You have certain feelings and certain circumstances.

You might be having a dream or two. Or a fantasy or a daydream.

You know you want to work this out – that's something you know.

But the way forward – the answer – it's just not clear at all.

This is a real state!

This is in process.

Transformation.

It's the thing before it looks like the thing.

We can let this be real. We have to let this be real.

Because flowers don't just appear – they sprout and grow and then bloom.

Laying out all the pieces, turning over all the stones… this collects into something.

In time.

The Limitations of Psychotherapy

Because of the range of types of therapy, it is difficult to speak about the limitations of psychotherapy specifically.

But there are limitations.

Each therapy is limited by the two people who do it.

You may benefit from complementary modalities such as naturopathy, massage, exercise, or spiritual work to address the issues you are bringing to therapy. Sometimes symptoms need to be managed in which case you may consider medication or therapies such as cognitive behavioural therapy or to complement your therapy.

You and your therapist can make a plan together or you may know intuitively what you need.

A final note: every profession has unethical and ineffective practitioners, and therapists are no different. If your therapist is acting in a way that makes you suspicious or unnerves you – talk to them about it. Follow your gut. While your feelings about your therapist are an important thing to work through, you have to feel safe with your therapist. You have to have faith that they are on your side. Without that, little will be accomplished.

Should you stay in therapy once the crisis that brought you there has passed?

You have made the leap and done the terrifying thing: you talked to a stranger about what is going on with you. About who you are. The initial crisis is, perhaps, over. You find yourself insisting to your therapist how you are not crazy, how everything is alright. You find yourself giving detailed updates of the week's events. You find yourself missing sessions. When your therapist's name comes through your inbox you cringe a bit. You have reached a crossroads.

It may be time to end therapy. Or – and I believe this is often although certainly not always the case – you have arrived at the point where the work is going to go somewhere difficult. It's not going to be easy and you know it. So you try to run away.

You have shown yourself to this person and now they might actually see you. And what will come of that?

Psychotherapy is in many ways a project of speaking. Can you put language to that fine line, that sliver of feeling, that your desire to flee sits on top of? Can you tell me what it is like for you to be exactly where you are? To be you, right now, having begun a process and wondering how it should continue?

I believe that a thoughtful answer to this question, developed over time, guides each of us to the next steps that are right for us. My advice is usually to listen to yourself. Do you believe that self-exploration will be valuable for you? Do you have the sense that there are feelings and thoughts just below the surface that, if unpacked, would lighten your load? This inner sense of knowing is an important underpinning of therapy. Without a sense that there is work to do or if you feel that your thoughts and feelings are better left unexplored therapy is perhaps not a good choice for you right now.

CHAPTER 5
FINAL THOUGHTS

Complementary Practices

Psychotherapy is one of many paths. I believe it is particularly well suited to the times in which we live.

And there are so many different ways to heal and grow. I often recommend that clients investigate other avenues alongside their therapy. And my personal journey has taken me in many directions. Each modality ads something unique and also universal.

As your therapy progresses, you might want to explore new ways of healing and growing. Having experiences where you have the opportunity for self-reflection in a different environment can provide insights that deepen your therapy in unexpected ways.

Within psychotherapy itself, there are many modalities to explore. Examples include art therapy, dream work, hypnotherapy, and EMDR. There are many others.

I often recommend naturopathic work alongside psychotherapy. Lifestyle, diet, and supplements to improve sleep and reduce stress can be very helpful when life is intense. Exercise in whatever form can be an important complement to therapy. Brain and body work together. Functional medicine takes naturopathy a step further – there are many cutting-edge alternative treatments that offer new perspectives and forms of healing.

Restorative yoga and meditation increase awareness and help you sink into your body. The body stores our experiences – it has been through everything that we remember and everything that we don't. Increasing our moment by moment awareness of our experience and moving into a deeper awareness of body sensation are both healing alongside psychotherapy. Some forms of psychotherapy involve these practices explicitly in sessions while some do them implicitly.

Bodywork is also a fruitful avenue for exploration and includes massage, cranial sacral therapy, Reiki, energy work, continuum, and somatic experiencing.

Writing is a practice you may find helpful. You can journal as a practice or just make notes in your phone when you have a dream or remember something you want to talk about in therapy. Writing catches who you are in different moments in time. Many of my clients read their writing to me in session.

The arts. Whether professional or amateur, the creative process is a core part of who we are. Artistic endeavours work beautifully alongside psychotherapy. If painting is something you have always wanted to do taking a class could bring up many useful insights alongside your work in therapy. And if you have an established artistic practice there may be much interplay between the work in therapy and your creative life.

These are a very small sample of the infinite possibilities. I find that clients who have other things they do during the week to support their growth get more out of their therapy. It is like they exercise the muscle more often so it becomes stronger.

And complementary modalities don't have to be new additions to your life. Whatever you enjoy is a practice of its own. Your creativity, generosity, physicality... these are all ways that you exercise your self. Exercising yourself is what therapy is all about. So what happens outside the room can build upon what happens in therapy and what happens in therapy can build on your other pursuits. Whatever they are.

What is emotional health?

Having a framework of what it is like to be healthy is important because it opens us up to what is possible. We are all pretty good at talking about problems – most people are familiar with anxiety, depression, narcissism, low self-esteem, etc. etc. etc. But we sometimes lack the language to talk about what it looks like to be a healthy human being.

STARTING THERAPY

Psychotherapy is not just about the relief of suffering. It is about living a good life. I find this notion to be little understood and certainly little discussed. Many clients leave therapy as soon as the crisis of suffering which brought them there has passed. In so doing I believe they walk away from what is available beyond the relief of suffering. This second part is harder work – it takes longer and often doesn't feel good in the short-term. But it is worth it. So worth it.

What is emotional health?[6]

1. The ability to regulate oneself, to pay attention, and to learn. Regulation is a crucial skill that many of us continually struggle to master. I think of the child who cries at their birthday party. The ability to calm ourselves down when we are excited, to soothe ourselves to sleep, to get the blood flowing when we feel sluggish – this is all about regulation. We need to regulate to be able to sustain our vitality throughout the day and then to be able to restore ourselves with sleep at night. The ability to focus and to learn is the result of a clear mind, unhampered by trauma and pain. We also need to regulate ourselves to have this focus.

Through therapy we gain a deeper sense of ourselves. Such that what happens out there in the world is not the definition of ourselves. We still have ups and downs, but there is a

---

[6] The following discussion of emotional health draws heavily from "The Profile Of Mental Functioning" in the Psychodynamic Diagnostic Manual, PDM Task Force, 2006.

something inside of us bigger than this. We don't believe that the truth is contained in each traffic jam or special present.

A grounded life of presence is possible. Most of the time.

2. The ability to experience, identify, and express emotions.

A wide range of them. Including the ones you'd rather not feel – whichever those are for you. For example, some people have difficulty accessing anger, others have difficulty accessing love. To be able to feel love, anger, joy, sadness, envy, and hope is all part of being a human being. Allowing ourselves to feel the feelings which we haven't allowed ourselves in the past can open up our emotional life and help us to feel calm and unburdened.

To be able to feel your feelings is a tremendous gift. It doesn't always feel good but to get the good emotions and experiences you have to work to withstand the bad.

For people in great emotional pain this sounds like a death sentence – particularly if your pain is an inwardly directed one based on past trauma or abuse. I am not saying that all therapy can offer is more of the same. Most likely there is some unfolding of your feelings possible. It's not just about bearing things.

But being able to notice, identify, and withstand your feelings directly, rather than move away into a preferred form of hiding is a huge benefit of therapy.

3. The capacity to have close relationships.

We are social beings and relationships matter. Every human being both needs and struggles in intimate relationships. The ability to sustain this struggle is a sign of health. This involves the ability to recognize the humanity of another person even when they have deeply wounded us. The ability to ask for help. The ability to speak of our experience even when it feels risky. The capacity to tolerate the ways in which those close to us do not meet our needs. Can we allow others to get close to us? Do we care about others? Do we have empathy for others?

It can be difficult to admit that one or more of your relationships are not what they could be. Sometimes it takes some work in therapy to discover this. And then some more to figure out what to do.

Therapy can help you have satisfying relationships with family, friends, lovers, colleagues, and acquaintances.

One of the ways that it helps is by helping you come in contact with your direct feelings. People are attracted to people who understand themselves. And people aren't attracted to people who swallow their emotions and let them come out in other less attractive ways. When someone appears inauthentic we don't trust them. People feel safe when they can sense that you feel safe in yourself. So as we change people's reactions to us also change.

That doesn't mean you don't feel angry, sad, envious or irritated with people. You will feel this often! But you feel the feelings directly and allow yourself to have them. You can feel the feelings without acting on them.

Everybody needs to be cherished. Deeply loved. Relationships with your inner circle can be a safe place to come "home" to. But many of us need to do some sorting out first. We need to figure out why certain relationships aren't working for us and we need to make some changes in ourselves and with our boundaries. We need to realize that a relationship isn't good just by virtue of existing – relationships involve effort. And relationships sometimes hurt.

All of this work can be done with the help of your therapist. And it starts with your relationship with him or her.

4. Realistic and reliable self-esteem.

When we have self-confidence we have a sense of well-being. We have energy. Healthy self-confidence is not unrealistic – we have a realistic sense of what we can do and what we can't do. We know that things get difficult and that we will experience times when our self-confidence is challenged. But we are confident enough to know that we bounce back. We can tolerate exploring our faults knowing that we are worthy, loved, and human.

5. The ability to self-reflect.

Self-reflection is the ability to think about ourselves. It requires a level of detachment from our feelings. No one is always perfectly detached. We all have times when we are overwhelmed by our feelings. But the ability to have that distance is an powerful way to improve our understanding of ourselves and our relationships.

6. Conscience.

Conscience is an inner sense of morality or values. It is the sense of a standard that we want to live up to. Conscience is internal rather than external. It allows us to feel appropriate guilt and to make reparations for our mistakes. Having a conscience is a sign that we are in relationship to others. That we have empathy for them and are balancing our needs with those of others.

7. Independence.

This is our freedom to act in the world. We know that the perceived or real expectations and desires of others are not the final word. They are not fact. We have something inside of us that must be reckoned with. This is our independence.

8. Object constancy.

Object constancy is the recognition that relationships continue despite physical distance. Children learn this in games such as peek-a-boo or hide and seek. When a parent is hiding we come to understand that they are still there. It allows us to know we are connected even when a loved one is preoccupied or tired. It allows us to remain confident in our connectedness and safety even when changing environments. It allows us to know that we can have those relationships, regardless of location.

9. The ability to allow our thoughts to inhibit our actions.

In moments of great feeling we may want to send an email, hit somebody, or cry. Sometimes emotional expression in the moment is exactly right. But sometimes we have to hold back. The ability to feel a feeling but not act on it because we know it is not the right thing to do (for us or for others) is evidence of emotional health.

10. Meaning.

Two areas where we find meaning are our families and our work lives.

Family

To have a stronger sense of self and what we need is a gift to our families. We can avoid upsets and blowouts by knowing what we need and what our families need and making good decisions individually and together.

Over time, a family with strong members who know their limits can love more deeply, more fiercely because they have access to all parts of their love.

I often get asked by my clients if a good relationship is possible. It's possible. Depending on your background you may have to fight like the devil to get it. But it's possible. And it starts with a regular practice devoted to your emotional health.

Work

Therapy can offer shifts in perspective about work that can be powerful. As you come to see yourself differently and as you come to understand your dynamic in relationship to others you will inevitably come to see your work life differently. You will come to a new understanding of your choices which can lead to more ownership over your life. From here – who knows what will happen?

11. Passion and vitality.

To have desire is to be alive. This means something different for each of us. What gets us going at the start of the day? What do we look forward to? Our connection to our vitality is our connection to meaning. It's our passion and our purpose. It's our "why."

Which leads to another possibility in therapy – increased energy and vitality. It takes a lot of energy to keep your feelings hidden and meet the perceived expectations of everyone else. As life goes on this takes more and more of you. The pressure increases when some other stressful event happens and the energy required to keep yourself together becomes greater. Being run down has to do with being busy. And with poor lifestyle choices. But it also has to do with the emotional activity required to maintain the status quo. Unpacking that emotional tightness and letting yourself go can result in vastly increased energy.

12. The capacity to mourn and surrender.

We cannot control everything. Our losses over a lifetime are great. The capacity to mourn and grieve, to recognize our losses and integrate them into our lives is an emotional achievement.

13. Recognition of vulnerability and dependency.

Plants breathe in carbon dioxide and exhale oxygen whereas humans breathe in oxygen and exhale carbon dioxide. Simplified as this is it makes an important point that we usually forget: we are completely dependent on each other and on the planet for our very survival. There is no such thing as being alone. The recognition of this makes for a realistic and wise human being.

14. The ability to be creative in the midst of suffering.

When we are going through something difficult it can be all-consuming. But there is humour and beauty at the most unexpected times. Can we find ourselves in our full range of feeling even when life is difficult? Can we allow suffering to crack us open in such a way that new strengths emerge? In such a way that we grow through the difficult times rather than stagnate?

15. Health

Repressed feelings are stored in our cells – they are stored in us. That's not a metaphor. Freeing up the flow of emotions is good for energy, sleep, stress, and overall health.

These are the possibilities. We can reach beyond symptom reduction, forward into a kind of living that has more room to breathe and light as well as dark.

This is important work

There is a lot of suffering in our world. The earth itself is suffering. We all have a responsibility to contribute in some way. Each of us has our own particular calling. But if we don't do our own work first we will often reinforce the wound which we seek to heal. We have to grow into ourselves and become flexible and strong. And then we can stand up for what is right and influence the world for good.

Think of the powerful people in the world who you believe have a destructive influence on something such as inequality, the health of the planet, or the well being of others. Imagine if those people knew their own worth, knew they were cherished, and could express their anger and joy freely and have it received. Then imagine what the world would be like with these differences. That is what I am talking about. And it starts with each of us.

Whatever life brings. And the life cycle brings each of us many things. Whatever life brings, the process of coming to know yourself will hold you in good stead. Because it never ends. We never "finish." So familiarity with yourself, care and respect for yourself, an awareness of how you impact others, an awareness of your work in the world and what it means to you – these things can guide you. These things can be treasures that continue to shine throughout your life. Therapy can change everything.

Therapy doesn't make us perfect. Therapy doesn't solve every problem. But it gives human beings the ability to access their own power and to be effective, compassionate and strong in their families, communities, and beyond. We need more real people who can withstand pain and anger and build the world we all want to live in. And the world we want to hand to our children. Therapeutic work can be a part of this. The importance of therapy is beyond mental health. Psychotherapy can help build the world that we want to live in.

RESOURCES

Recommended Reading

Addiction to Perfection: The Still Unravished Bride: A Psychological Study, Marion Woodman

The Body Keeps the Score: Brain, Mind, and Body in the Healing of Trauma, Bessel Van Der Kolk

Daring Greatly: How the Courage to Be Vulnerable Transforms the Way We Live, Love, Parent, and Lead, Brené Brown

The Drama of the Gifted Child: The Search for the True Self, Alice Miller

I'm Working On It In Therapy: How To Get the Most Out Of Psychotherapy, Gary Trosclair

In the Realm of Hungry Ghosts: Close Encounters With Addiction, Gabor Maté

Understanding and Healing Emotional Trauma: Conversations With Pioneering Clinicians and Researchers, Daniela Sieff

Writing

The Artist's Way, Julia Cameron

Writing Down the Bones: Freeing the Writer Within, Natalie Goldberg

Writing the Mind Alive: The Proprioceptive Method for Finding Your Authentic Voice, Linda Trichter Metcalf

Yoga and Meditation

How to Meditate: A Practical Guide to Making Friends With Your Mind, Pema Chödrön

Yoga for Emotional Flow, Audio CD, Stephen Cope

Yoga for Depression: A Compassionate Guide to Relieve Suffering Through Yoga, Amy Weintraub

ACKNOWLEDGEMENTS

A heart felt thank you to all my individual therapists over the years: Karen, Judith, Kim, Anna, Sharlene, Judith, and Cynthia. Thank you as well to the group and couples therapists and the other healers in so many other disciplines who have contributed to my growth. Thank you to my supervisors and in particular my ongoing supervisor Sharon who helps me form into the therapist and person who I am. I know both the challenge and the reward of this work and am grateful that so many people have given of themselves in their work with me.

Thank you to my blog readers. You encourage me to write by your interest, your openness, and your direct encouragement.

Thank you to Francesca for the early editing and Lynne for the copyediting and shepherding me through the launch. Lynne you are a rock of my work and I am so grateful for you.

To my husband Paul – thank you for always being interested in my writing. For long conversations while we look out over trees and lakes and wonder what this work is that we do. I wouldn't have written this without you.

Twokay the cat – thank you for not understanding a word of any of this. You give me much needed perspective and snuggles.

Finally – thank you to my clients. Each of you brings me something uniquely yours. The work we do is precious to me. Through the hours we have spent together I have written these words. You are a part of this writing and I am grateful for your presence in my life in this and so many other ways.

Alison Crosthwait first entered a therapist's office in 1993. Over the past 25 years, she has studied and experienced therapy in many forms as both therapist and client. She is the author of a weekly blog on Psychotherapy and offers a free email course on getting the most out of your therapy. Both can be found at www.thegoodtherapists.com.

Made in the USA
San Bernardino, CA
23 December 2017